RAISING PURITY

Nurturing the image of God
in the heart of your child

GERALD HIESTAND

RAISING PURITY

*Nurturing the image of God
in the heart of your child*

GERALD HIESTAND

RYVER MEDIA
Pingree Grove, Illinois

RAISING PURITY: NURTURING THE IMAGE OF GOD
IN THE HEART OF YOUR CHILD

Unless otherwise noted, all Scripture quotations are from the Holy Bible, New International Version (North American Edition). Copyright © 1973, 1978, 1984 by International Bible Society. Used by permission of Zondervan Publishing House. Any emphasis indicated is the author's.

Scripture quotations marked NASB are from the New American Standard Bible, copyright © 1960, 1962, 1963, 1968, 1971, 1972, 1973, 1975, 1977 by The Lockman Foundation. Used by permission. Any emphasis indicated is the author's.

Scripture quotations marked RSV are from the Revised Standard Version of the Bible, copyright © 1946, 1952, 1971, 1973 by the Division of Christian Education of the National Council of Churches of Christ in the U.S.A. Used by permission.

Cover and interior design: Eric Spragg

Address all inquiries to:
info@ryvermedia.com

TO JACOB THOMAS AND NATHAN JAMES

CONTENTS

PREFACE

Throughout this book's three-year development, its pages have undergone so many revisions that I can scarcely remember them all. In many ways this book's slow evolution has mirrored my own journey toward a deeper grasp of sexual purity. Through it all I have learned that true purity is found not in the mastering of one's will but in the mastering of one's desires. Someone once said that those who protest most loudly about a given vice are often themselves most vulnerable to that vice. Such a sentiment has not been lost on me, and I readily admit that my initial desire to write about sexual purity stemmed in part from my own quest for the same. And though my journey is not complete, it is with deep thankfulness to God that the completion of this book finds me far beyond the place where I was when it began.

Perhaps the biggest difference between this final version of the book and the earlier versions is its emphasis upon the gospel. Great theologians throughout history have often talked about the difference between Law and gospel. Law, they have said, is what we should do. Gospel, on the other hand, is the power to do it. The Christian must have both. Without the Law, we do not know how we are to live. Without the gospel, we do not possess the power to live according to what we know. My earlier versions of this book emphasized the Law but were short on the gospel. This was true of the book partly because it was true in my life.

But I have since learned that God's grace is not only the freedom of forgiveness but also the blessings of power, of new life, and of transformed desires. God, being rich in mercy, has made us alive with Christ and has begun the work of transforming our sinful hearts after the image of His Son. And with this new heart comes holy desires. This book stands as a testimony to the overpowering goodness of the grace of God, a grace that can transform the hearts of sinful individuals and cause them to delight in holiness even more than they delight in sin.

I want to thank the many people who have helped with this project: Barb Pierce, whose careful reading of my manuscript was of great value in bringing out many issues that I had neglected to originally include, as well as excluding items that were superfluous; Bill Edmondson of Ryver Media, who resurrected this project when I had all but moved on; Eric Spragg, for his help with the graphic design; Melissa Meyer, for her proofing and having an eye for the details; Jason Barbieri and David Hill for reading through early versions of the manuscript; and the many friends at Fremont Evangelical Free Church, Fremont, Nebraska, where the initial bulk of the writing was done. And most significantly, I am deeply grateful to my wife, Jill, who has been both an encouragement to me and a model of grace throughout our eight years of marriage.

—Gerald Hiestand, September 2005

The Need to Know Why

Searching for Clarity

---

*"Just as he who called you is holy, so be holy in all
you do; for it is written:'Be holy, because I am holy.'"*
—*The Apostle Peter*

Welcome. I invite you on a journey—a journey into the heart of purity
and the image of God. We will not be searching for an empty moralism—a
pharisaical, legalistic list of dos and don'ts. We will not be seeking after out-
ward obedience devoid of heartfelt submission. We will not be looking to
control our children for our own ends, nor even to spare them from harm.
On this journey we will be searching for the heart of God, expressed fully
in the person of Christ. We will be searching for a Son-exalting purity that
is not defined by what it isn't but by what it *is*. Ultimately—though perhaps
you didn't realize it—we will be searching for the gospel.

But before we can raise up a *spirit* of purity in the hearts of our children, we must first raise up a *picture* of purity that is clear, obtainable, and
knowable. Such a picture, I believe, has been lost in much of the church
today. Do we know what God-centered purity looks like beside the external
commands regarding premarital sex and adultery? Can we speak with certainty and clarity—indeed with divine authority—about how our children
should relate sexually to members of the opposite sex? Or is the advice we
give merely the sum total of our own wisdom, derived loosely from Biblical
principles and our past experience? What is purity? What does it look like,
and what lies at its heart? Why should we even care? These are the questions we will seek to answer on our journey.

But why another book on sexual purity? Will your time spent here be worth the investment? I believe so. This book, unlike others, ties together sexual purity with the image of the gospel. To my knowledge, this connection has not been explored at length nor applied to our contemporary Christian culture. Many books on sex, dating, and purity instruct on right behavior, but I have seen an absence of books that adequately explain *why* God commands such behavior.

I believe the answer to this "why" question is rooted squarely in the interconnectedness of sex, the gospel, and the image of God. When we help our children understand the "why" of God's commands, we inevitably testify to the glorious truth of the gospel, we nurture a heart of purity, and we eliminate for our children much of the subjectivity that would otherwise surround this issue.

For You, the Parent

Unlike many books that address issues of sexuality, dating, and romance, this work is directed primarily toward the parent. As a former youth pastor, I have observed firsthand just how important parental influence is. For a child to grow straight and true when the parents are crooked and bent is a miracle of divine intervention. It can and does happen, for this is the power of the gospel, but the normal and natural course of spiritual nurturing in the life of a child reflects the dependency of a positive parent-child relationship. It is the parent's job, even before the church's job, to "train a child in the way he should go." My primary aim, therefore, is to help you as a parent understand God's perspective on sexual purity, for if it is not clear to you, it will likely not be clear to your children. We as parents can give only what we possess.

Further, the principles prescribed in this book (and, I believe, in the Word of God) are fairly conservative compared to the views of much of our current Christian culture. This is perhaps the most significant reason I have chosen to address parents as the primary audience. Many students I have taught have understood the truths of God's Word and have given verbal assent to the direction advised here. But intellectual assent and willful obedience are not the same thing. Because many parents do not question the status quo of our culture, young people often find it difficult to choose a conservative path. Christian young people have an incredible ability to live for God, but we as parents must do everything we can to protect this desire and bring it to fruition.

It is important to mention from the outset that this book is not only for those of you who have children just entering the preteen years but also for future parents and those whose children have yet to begin thinking about the opposite sex. If you are part of this latter group, you have a tremendous opportunity to begin guiding your children's expectations toward a godly path. Your children, will develop expectations. Will they develop them based upon what they see on television, hear from their friends, or read in books? Or will their expectations be shaped by the Word of God?

DEFINING AND APPLYING SEXUAL PURITY

Though two chapters of this book address the subject of dating, the focus of this book is not really about dating, courtship, or how to find a spouse. I have intentionally limited myself to the simple aim of clarifying and applying the nature of sexual purity. I touch upon these other topics only as they relate to this central aim.

Further, unlike many books on sexual purity, this book does not contain a host of data carefully detailing the repercussions of sexual immorality. An approach to sexual purity that uses the fear of STDs, unwanted pregnancies, and emotional scars as a means of motivating a child to remain sexually pure is based upon the faulty assumption that God's commands exist solely for our own protection. Though it is true that God's commands do protect us from harm, Scripture makes it quite clear that God's commands are not about what works best for us but about what brings him the most glory. Consequently we will not be relying on the "fear factor" as we seek to help our children strive for a life of purity.

As we will see, God has created the sexual relationship between a man and a woman to be a living image of the gospel. It is this truth that provides the "why" of all of God's commands and acts as the primary motivator that he sets forth for a life of obedience. As we explore the topic of sexual purity, we will learn that God calls our children to sexual purity, not because it is good for them (though it *is* good for them), but rather because through the proper use of our sexuality, we portray a picture of salvation—a deep and profound image of the gospel.

CONCLUSION

So, parents, this book is for you—that you may have clarity in your heart and mind about what God has ordained as appropriate within male/female relationships and that you will pass along to your children a clear picture of purity, enabling them to grow into young people who honor God with their sexuality.

For too long we have allowed our young people to wander aimlessly in their search for godliness in the arena of sexual purity. The road is long for both parent and child—longer perhaps than when you and I had to travel it. It is wrought with pitfalls and moral hazards that threaten destruction and death, both literally and spiritually. I know that you long to see your children succeed. You long for their good and their happiness. God longs for this as well, and he promises a good return for our investment of faith.

As you read through this book, I challenge you to think carefully about how well our current culture fits with what Scripture teaches about the connection between sexuality and the image of God. It is my prayer that above all God will use at least some of what I have written here to bring clarity and focus to that image, that the glory and image of the gospel might be seen ever more clearly in the lives of our children. May he turn our children's gray world of relativity into a black-and-white world of Christ-honoring sexual purity!

Chapter 1

SEX AND THE GOSPEL

PORTRAYING OUR UNION WITH THE DIVINE NATURE

"[Christ is] united to you by a spiritual union, so close as to be fitly represented by the union of the wife to the husband."

—Jonathan Edwards

"... Adam, ... a type of Him who was to come."
—The Apostle Paul (NASB)

We are a people fascinated with sex.

Men and women, young and old. Christians, atheists, and everyone in between. In all cultures, throughout all of history, sexual desire has been one of the greatest motivators of the human will. Men and women throw away their families, houses, money, and land in order to be sexually satisfied. Some are addicted to it. Wars have been fought over it. We compose songs about it, make movies about it, and write stories about it. And this preoccupation with sex is not simply a facet of our fallen nature. Even one whole book of the Bible is dedicated to celebrating the sexual relationship between the husband and wife.

But have you ever wondered why all the fuss? Why did God create us as sexual people in the first place? I remember learning in science class about the asexual reproduction of single-celled organisms and being grateful that God had chosen a different method of reproduction for humans. The thought of mitosis didn't (and still doesn't) sound as appealing as the method of reproduction that God gave us. But why did God choose to create us as sexual beings? He was obviously not tied to a need for sexual reproduction in order to propagate the species. He just as easily could have created humans as asexual creatures that reproduced like amoebas.

Until we understand why God created sex, we will never sufficiently make sense of his commands regarding sexual purity, for his commands always relate to his purposes. So to establish a biblical understanding of sexual purity, this chapter is dedicated to capturing a biblical understanding of sex itself.

LAYING THE FOUNDATION: UNDERSTANDING THE PURPOSE OF SEX

The primary reason that many of us do not adequately understand sex is because we do not adequately understand how sex relates to the gospel. As we will see, sex and the gospel are intrinsically linked. To understand one is to make sense of the other.

Shocking though this may seem, Scripture expressly states that God created sex to serve as a living witness of the life-changing union that believers have with God through Christ. Understanding how sex serves this function is absolutely essential for understanding not only why God created us as sexual beings but also why God commands what he does regarding sexual purity. Ultimately, we will discover that God created the physical oneness of sex to serve as a visible image, or type, of the spiritual union that exists between Christ and the church. Though it may seem at first that we are diverging far from the primary topic of sexual purity, you will quickly see the significance of our discussion.

> *Sex and the gospel are intrinsically linked. To understand one is to make sense of the other.*

"TYPES" IN THE BIBLE

Two of history's greatest theologians, Jonathan Edwards and Augustine, built much of their theology upon the idea that the image of God and his purposes can be seen in all facets of human existence. Both theologians believed that God created all of life to serve as visible portraits of invisible realities. To see the love between a father and his son, for example, is to see a reflection of the love between God the Father and God the Son. To see the destruction caused by fire is to see a picture of the wrath of God. To see the creativity of an artist is to see a reflection of the creativity of God.[1]

Seeing earthly entities as pictures of divine realities is readily affirmed in much of Scripture. Romans 5:14 (NASB), for example, describes Adam as a "type" of Christ. The word "type" comes from the Greek word *tupos,* which literally means "blow" or "impression" and refers to the indentation a hammer creates after it strikes wood or metal. Often translated in the New Testament as "example," a *tupos* is a model or image of something.

> *Sex within marriage is a living picture of the gospel.*

Just as an indentation represents that which made it, so too a *tupos* points to, or represents, something other than itself. Adam, then, is a shadow, or an image of Christ. Adam's existence points us toward that which he represents—namely Christ.

Scripture is replete with such analogies. Hebrews 11:19 refers to Isaac as a type of Christ, for just as Abraham received him back from certain death, so too we have received Christ back from the dead. The atoning death of a lamb in the Old Testament foreshadowed the atoning death of the Lamb of God in the New Testament. Melchizedek's mysterious priesthood was a picture of the eternal Priesthood of Christ. In Galatians Paul used Isaac and Ishmael as representatives of two contrasting covenants (the New and the Old). As we will see from Scripture, just as Adam served as a living *tupos,* or image, of Christ, so too sex has been created by God to serve as a living image of the gospel. In other words, when we think of sex, we should ultimately think of the gospel.

FOR THIS REASON

Ephesians 5:28–32 pointedly describes the sexual relationship within marriage as an image of the spiritual relationship between Christ and the church. As you read the passage, note carefully the significance of the last sentence (verse 32) within its context.[2]

> Even so husbands should love their wives as their own
> bodies. He who loves his wife loves himself. For no man

ever hates his own flesh, but nourishes and cherishes it, as Christ does the church, because we are members of his body. "For this reason a man shall leave his father and mother and be joined to his wife [i.e., sexual intercourse], and the two shall become one flesh." This mystery is a profound one, and I am saying that it refers to Christ and the church [RSV].

In this passage Paul is talking about Christ's relationship with the church, stating that Christ cares for us because we are members of his body, just as a wife's body is the body of her husband. Paul then inserts a passage from Genesis 2, beginning with the phrase "For this reason." He includes this phrase to demonstrate that the sexual relationship within marriage exists for the sake of the "heavenly marriage." Don't miss this! Essentially Paul is saying, "Because of the spiritual relationship that exists between Christ and his church, . . . for this reason a man leaves his father and mother and cleaves to his wife, and the two become one flesh" (RSV).[3] In other words, sexual oneness within marriage exists as an image of the spiritual oneness between Christ and the church.

Paul makes this even clearer in verse 32, where he specifically states that the mystery of a man and a woman becoming one flesh refers to Christ and the church. From this passage we can see that the physical union that results from sexual intercourse is akin to the spiritual union between Christ and the church.

The apostle Paul states that when a man and a woman come together sexually, in some mysterious way they "become one" in their flesh (Ephesians 5:31; 1 Corinthians 6:16). Something profound occurs through sexual intercourse. The union is not simply a legal union but rather a union of bodies, a sharing of physical life. Two people are joined together in the deepest and most wonderful way. This union is then to be lived out through the course of a permanent marriage relationship and explains why a husband is to lovingly care for his wife: because she has become one flesh with him. To care for her is to care for himself (Ephesians 5:28). A marriage relationship is the "living out" of the

> *The fact that the oneness of sex images the oneness of our spiritual relationship with Christ is not merely a happy coincidence.*

union that is established by the oneness of sexual intercourse. (This is why a sexual relationship that occurs outside the context of a marriage relationship is so destructive. The act of sex, which is meant to initiate a permanent union, is broken apart.)

But herein lies the significance of sex—not what it accomplishes on an earthly plane but what it images forth on a divine plane. It is not an end in itself; it is a type of something higher, pointing to the deeper reality of the gospel. Just as sex establishes a new union between a man and a woman and explains the shared life that follows, so too the indwelling of the Holy Spirit marks a new union between Christ and the Christian and accounts for the life-change that follows. Just as a husband and wife "become one" physically, Christ

> *When we "become one" spiritually with Christ himself, we enter into both forgiveness and life.*

and the Christian "become one" spiritually. The New Testament's many references to the church as the "bride" of Christ and to Christ as the "bridegroom" support this parallel between earthly and heavenly union. Further, many of Christ's parables use the wedding motif as an illustration of his return and consummate union with the church. And Revelation explicitly refers to the wedding of the Lamb and the church as inaugurating the dawn of the eternal age (Matthew 25:1–13; Revelation 19:7; 21:2, 9; 22:17).[4]

When we think of sexual oneness between a man and a woman as an image, or type, of our spiritual oneness with Christ, it is important to remember which came first in God's mind. God did not pattern the divine marriage after human marriage, but rather human marriage is a picture of the divine marriage. The fact that the oneness of sex images the oneness of our spiritual relationship with Christ is not merely a happy coincidence. Just as God ordained the Passover lamb of the Old Covenant to prophetically witness to the coming sacrifice of Christ, so too God ordained human marriage to testify to the coming wedding supper of the Lamb.

REMEMBERING THE GOSPEL

Our spiritual union with Christ is an essential yet often overlooked aspect of the gospel. That lapse is, I believe, the primary reason the church has largely failed to see the illustrative relationship between sex and salvation. A brief restatement of the gospel is in order. The good news of salvation is not simply that God has forgiven us, but rather that through our union with Christ we are born again into his very life—we have become sharers of his nature (2 Peter 1:4). Forgiveness is indeed a significant aspect of our salvation, but we must not reduce the saving work of God to simple bookkeeping in the divine registry, cleaning out our account of sins but otherwise leaving us untouched.[5] Forgiveness cleans the slate, but forgiveness alone is not sufficient for entering the kingdom of Heaven.

That last sentence is worth repeating. Forgiveness alone is not sufficient for entering the kingdom of Heaven. When we understand that our chief culpability before God is not bound up in our sinful actions but even more fundamentally in our sinful nature—the source of our sinful actions—we can begin to understand why we need more than forgiveness.

Not surprisingly, the main requirement for entering into eternal life is that one actually be alive. Jesus himself said, " 'No one can see [enter into] the kingdom of God unless he is born again' " (John 3:3). The essence of our New Testament salvation, therefore, is our connection to the very life of God, through Jesus Christ by the indwelling presence of the Holy Spirit. It is when we "become one" spiritually with Christ himself that we enter into both forgiveness and life. Just as a husband and wife become one in their physical life, so too Christ and the Christian, through the indwelling of the Spirit, become one in their spiritual life. Through our union with him, his life has become our own. We are born again precisely because we have been united to the One who is Life itself.

> *Through our union with Christ, we have been blessed with every spiritual blessing.*

The ability to live a God-pleasing life, indeed to inherit eternal life, does not stem from our dedication to God or vows of our will; rather it flows from the divine life granted to us through our supernatural union with Christ. The very life of God through Christ via the Holy Spirit has taken up residence inside us. We are irrevocably wed to the divine nature, and human marriage is yet another powerful picture, or symbol, of this union.

In the end, our final hope of salvation is that we have been "married" to Christ. When we come to God for salvation, he makes us one with Christ—just as a man and a woman become one in marriage. This union with Christ is the very thing that provides eternal life. Indeed, the eternal life that we have now begun to live is the eternal life that Christ lives. The sap of the vine is the sap of the branch. Through our union with him, we have been blessed with every spiritual blessing (Ephesians 1:3). He has become our head, and his job is to present us "to himself as a radiant church, without stain or wrinkle or any other blemish, but holy and blameless" (Ephesians 5:27). And he will do it. Marriage and sex are powerful illustrations of this union that exists between Christ and the Christian, and they were created specifically for that purpose.

The "Why" and the "How" of Sexual Purity

Now that we understand why God created sex, we can begin to understand the reasons behind his commands regarding sexual purity. Ultimately, God's commands always relate to his image.

We tend to believe that God's commands are given to us merely for our own sake. But this is not true. As those created in the image of God, our very nature as image-bearers explains the reason behind God's commands. Not only is sex a divine type of the gospel, man himself is a type of God (Genesis 1:26, 27; Romans 8:29–31; 1 Corinthians 11:7; 15:49). Since God created us to be images, or types, of himself, revealing his invisible glory to the visible world, it is essential that all we do be aligned with all that God does, for we glorify God by manifesting his goodness through our own goodness. Our glory is his glory, for the glory and goodness we possess is not inherent within us but comes first from him, testifying to his infinite goodness.

> *Every action to which we are called relates to God's actions and nature.*

Therefore, the ways in which God acts, loves, thinks, and feels all provide the basis for how we are to act, love, think, and feel. We are called to act mercifully because he is merciful (Luke 6:36); we are called to be perfect because he is perfect (Mathew 5:48); we are called to do good to our enemies because he does good to his (Mathew 5:44, 45); and we are called to be holy because he is holy (1 Peter 1:15, 16). Ultimately, every action to which we are called, every function that he created us to fulfill, relates to God's actions and nature. This is no less true regarding sex and God's commands for sexual purity.

God's major intent in creating sex was that it serve as a living witness of the spiritual reality of Christ's oneness with the church. Knowledge of this higher reality then helps us understand how we should behave within the realm of the earthly reality. In other words, our sex lives should be patterned after the way in which Christ and the church relate spiritually. Viewing sexuality from this framework not only explains how we should act but also why we should act a certain way.

For example, in 1 Corinthians 6:15–17, the commands that Paul gives regarding sexual activity are based on the "one spirit" relationship between Christ and the church. We must not unite ourselves sexually to a prostitute,

> *We were made to be like God, existing as living portraits of his divine goodness.*

Paul argues, because we have become united spiritually to Christ. But the prohibition in this passage is not against sex in general but against sex with a prostitute. Our spiritual oneness with Christ does not prevent us from having sex with our spouse. In fact, Paul commands this in 1 Corinthians 7:5. But why is sex with our spouse righteous and sex with a prostitute sinful? How is it that our spiritual oneness with Christ does not stand in the way of all sexual relationships?

When talking to your children about the importance of sexual purity, it is tempting to answer their questions on a strictly human level. We might list the myriad of sexually transmitted diseases that can be caught. We could list documented adverse psychological effects of promiscuity. We could talk further about the negative effects of sexual licentiousness on one's future spouse or the possibility of an unwanted pregnancy. But all of these issues only reinforce the idea that sex is all about us, as though God's commands have only to do with what works best for humanity. Even apart from such side effects promiscuous sex would still be forbidden. None of these matters, however true, get to the root of why God has forbidden sex with a prostitute. The issue must first be addressed on a divine plane before it can be addressed on a human plane.

As we saw, God's commands relate to the image of the heavenly realities that he intends our lives to bear. Sex with a prostitute then is forbidden because it breaks the picture of Christ's single-minded connection and devotion to his Bride. Just as Christ reserves himself spiritually for his spouse (the church), so too we are called to reserve ourselves sexually for our

> *We are not our own. . . . Our image belongs to Christ.*

husband or wife. The way we behave sexually must conform to that which God has created sex to illustrate: the life-changing nature of the gospel. Monogamy and permanency are vital aspects of this image. Christ is united to the church alone, thus a man must be united to his wife alone. Christ does not divorce his Bride. We must not divorce our spouse.

The young man who uses his sexuality in a promiscuous way does not act consistently with the image of Christ's monogamous wait for his Bride. Christ has purposed to become one with only the church. So too must young people reserve their sexuality for their future spouses as an expression of Christ's single-minded devotion to his own. God calls us to reserve our sexuality for the marriage relationship, because it is only in marriage that the image of Christ's relationship to the church can be lived out.

It is fundamentally important that we teach our children to act out their sexually in a manner consistent with the image that it was created to portray. We will explore the full implications of this in chapters to come, particularly as it relates to establishing an objective definition of sexual purity.[6]

CONCLUSION

We were made to be like God, existing as living portraits of his divine goodness. Every task that God gives us is centered on his own purposes and nature. Human government, marriage, sex, parents, and Christians themselves (to name just a few) all relate to God's purposes and actions, serving as images of higher heavenly realities. God is about glorifying himself, and the way he has chosen to do so in our lives is

> *It is only when we live out the image of God that we will find the happiness of God.*

through our existence in his glorious image. Like an earthly father who is glorified through the glory of his children, so too God is glorified through our glorification (Romans 8:30). But such glory cannot be achieved apart from our living out the image of God, for only in God himself is true glory found.

This is why our lives are not about ourselves alone. We are not our own. We bear the image of another, and the ownership of that image belongs to him. And since we bear the image of another, we are not free to decide for ourselves what is best for us. We must not act in ways that are inconsistent with the character of the One we portray. It is important that we live every facet of our lives as a correct witness to the image of God. Everything that he asks of us, he asks so we might be conformed to his image.

As we study sexual purity, we must remember that every part of us, including our sexuality, has a higher purpose than merely our own pleasure, for every part of us was created primarily to image forth the glory of God. When we learn to view the world as a mirror of God's own divine nature and purposes, we are saved from the dead end of self-absorption; life has a higher purpose than our own autonomous satisfaction.

As we have seen, God has ordained sex that through it we might see a living illustration of the gospel, our union with the divine nature. Though our children may not be old enough to understand this truth on a cognitive level, we can begin to teach it to them on a subjective level by how we live out our own sexuality. We must teach our children, through word and example, that they are not their own, that they have been bought with a price, and, therefore, must honor God with their bodies. He desires their best. He desires their sexual satisfaction more than they ever will, for through the proper expression of their sexuality, both they and the world will have a lens through which to see the heart of the gospel. If they grow to believe the lie that sex is about their own happiness alone, they will be robbed of the joy that God intends it to bring. For it is only when we live out the image of God that we will find the happiness of God.

Discussion Questions

What is a "type"? What are some examples of types in the Bible?

According to Ephesians 5:28–32, how does sex serve as a type, or image, of the gospel?

What happens when a man and woman come together sexually? How is this like Christ's relationship to the church?

How does knowing that God created sex to serve as a living image of our union with Christ help us understand the reason behind God's commands regarding sexual purity?

What applications can be drawn from the fact that God created sex to serve as a type of Christ and the church, particularly in the realm of sexual satisfaction and sexual purity? (See Appendix B.)

Chapter 2

MORE THAN
A SUBJECTIVE STANDARD

PURITY AND THE GOD-ORDAINED CATEGORIES
OF MALE/FEMALE RELATIONSHIPS

*"Treat younger men as brothers, older women as
mothers, and younger women as sisters, with absolute
purity."*

—The Apostle Paul

This book originated out of my desire to arrive at a biblical, objective definition of sexual purity—a sexual purity of both body and heart. And though there is much more to purity than how we behave, our behavior is a tangible expression of our inward devotion. Christian piety and holiness cannot be separated from external obedience. We are both body and

> *Our behavior is a tangible
> expression of our inward devotion.*

spirit, flesh and soul, and God has given us an external standard of holiness so we can catch a visible glimpse of the invisible inward purity of the heart. Though purity of body cannot be the end-all of Christlikeness, it nonetheless provides a reference point from which to launch a discussion regarding purity of heart.

Consequently, I have two main objectives for the next three chapters. The first is to establish from Scripture a biblical, objective definition of external sexual purity, binding for all people in all circumstances. The second is to examine current dating practices in light of this biblical definition. It is my conviction that the current dating paradigm that permeates Christian culture is largely responsible for much of the confusion today regarding sexual purity. If you have become weary of "kissing dating good-bye," I invite you to lend an open mind.

By way of introduction, allow me to introduce you to "Miss Average Student," a sixteen-year old in the local evangelical youth group. She will help us navigate the muddied waters of today's teen culture.

Gerald: So I hear you have a new boyfriend.

Student: Yeah, Tom and I have been going out now for three weeks.

Gerald: Really? How's that been going for you?

Student: It's been going great. We have so much in common. I can already tell that we're really going to hit it off.

Gerald: Well, I certainly hope so. Do you mind if I ask you something a little personal?

Student: Umm . . . I guess you can.

Gerald: I was just wandering what your physical relationship is like. I mean, does Tom kiss you?

Student: I . . . err . . . I don't know.

Gerald: You don't know, or you don't want to say?

Student: I don't want to say.

Gerald: Why don't you want to say? Is there something wrong with kissing?

Student: There's nothing wrong with kissing. I mean, there could be something wrong with kissing if two people were, like, *really* kissing. But if you're just kissing, it's not that big of a deal.

Gerald: How do you know that *really* kissing is bad and "just kissing" is fine?

Student: Well, you have to be careful, because if you get carried away, you can start doing things you shouldn't.

Gerald: But how do you know what kinds of things you shouldn't do?

Student: (*pauses*) I guess I'm not totally sure. I mean, I know you shouldn't have sex . . .

Gerald: Well, I'll mention some other things, and you tell me if you think they are okay or not. How about holding hands?

Student: That's fine.

Gerald: How about a good-night kiss?

Student: Fine.

Gerald: A prolonged good-night kiss, but not a French kiss.

Student: That's fine.

Gerald: How about a lot of kissing, say fifteen minutes worth, but still no French kissing?

Student: I guess that's okay.

Gerald: How about French kissing?

Student: Maybe, but that's it.

Gerald: Why?

Student: I just wouldn't feel comfortable doing anything more than that.

Gerald: So do you determine what is right based on what you feel comfortable with?

Student: Well, I guess. Each person has to pray about it and come to his or her own standard of how far is too far. For myself, I just wouldn't want to do any more than that.

Gerald: What if you had a friend who felt comfortable with French kissing and caressing. As long as she felt comfortable, would that be okay?

Student: Well, the guy she's with might not feel comfortable. Maybe that would be too tempting for him and would make him want to do more than he should.

Gerald: What do you mean by "more than he should"? How do we know how far is too far for him?

Student: He needs to know that for himself, I guess.

Gerald: Okay then. Let's say that both the guy and the girl feel comfortable with heavy French kissing and caressing. Is it okay, since they both feel comfortable with what they're doing?

Student: *(pauses)* Well, I don't think that would be right . . .

Gerald: Neither do I, but how would you convince them that they are doing something inappropriate?

Student: I guess I'm not really sure.

So how far is too far, anyway? I can recall sitting with my youth minister over breakfast and discussing the issue of purity between dating couples. With me were four or five students my own age, some who had grown up in the church and others who came from unchurched families. We all believed that the Bible clearly prohibited sex before marriage (though I don't think we could have found the Bible's chapter and verse to back up our view), but our convictions did not reach far beyond that.

> *So how far is too far, anyway?*

My youth minister agreed that indeed the Bible does prohibit sex before marriage, but unfortunately, since dating is not specifically mentioned in the Bible, we needed to come to our own conclusions about what was physically appropriate in a dating relationship. So each of us in turn sounded off with whatever our seventeen-year-old wisdom could muster. Our answers ranged from "prolonged kissing" to "as long as the clothes stay on."

I remember my youth minister cautioning against the more liberal standards, using the argument that it is hard to stop short of sex when things have progressed. He also cautioned us against the danger of lust, which can often accompany even light sexual interaction, and he mentioned the need to be pure. But he did not say that such boundaries were wrong. In the end he had no objective standard of purity with which to advise us. Instead he encouraged us each to prayerfully come to our own convictions about what was physically appropriate in a dating relationship and to follow the leading of the Holy Spirit. Ultimately we were left to seek our own wisdom.

The track my youth minister took seems to be the conventional wisdom in much of the literature I have read on this topic. Though giving a great deal of otherwise excellent advice regarding sexual purity, one author ends his chapter "How far is too far?" by stating,

You may want me to tell you, in much more detail, exactly what's right for you when it comes to secular boundaries. But in the end, you have to stand before God. That's why you must set your own boundaries according to His direction for your life.... [To] keep my mind and body pure, I chose not to kiss [my wife] until the day we were engaged.... I'm not saying this has to be one of your boundaries too. I want you to build your own list of sexual standards.[1]

But do we really want our children to build their own lists of sexual standards? I would argue that adolescents are no more qualified to build their own lists of sexual standards than young children are qualified to decide for themselves how much candy is too much. Even we adults are often not mature enough to seek our own wisdom regarding sexual purity.

Right from Wrong: How Much Do Our Children Know?

My experience as a young person was not unique. Beyond the prohibition of extramarital sex, many (if not most) young people today do not have objective biblical standards regarding the issue of purity. They need a clear, quantifiable picture of purity that originates from the Word of God, and they need to understand why God has set the standard he has.

The book, *Right from Wrong,* by Josh McDowell and Bob Hostetler, highlights the confusion that is rampant among young people today regarding sexual mores. The book covers a wide range of topics, gathering information through careful surveys that document the extent to which Christian young people from evangelical churches discern right from wrong. In the book McDowell and Hostetler deal extensively with the issue of sexual purity, and their study reveals disturbing facts. The following two charts from their book demonstrate the confusion that many young people feel today regarding the whole issue of sexual purity.[2]

Activity	Always	Sometimes	Never	Not Sure
Holding hands	85%	14%	1%	1%
Embracing and some kissing	68%	29%	2%	1%
Heavy "French" kissing	33%	48%	11%	9%
Fondling of breasts	10%	25%	49%	16%
Fondling of genitals	9%	20%	55%	16%
Sexual intercourse	7%	13%	68%	12%

Table B-3.1, Right from Wrong

ACTIVITIES DEEMED MORALLY ACCEPTABLE
AND THE INCIDENCE OF SUCH BEHAVIOR

Activity	Morally Acceptable	Engaged in This Activity
Holding hands	99%	88%
Embracing and some kissing	97%	72%
Heavy "French" kissing	80%	51%
Fondling of breasts	36%	33%
Fondling of genitals	30%	25%
Sexual intercourse	20%	15%

Table B-3.2, Right from Wrong

Table B-3.2 is particularly concerning. According to McDowell and Hostetler, the vast majority of Christian young people (80 percent) believe that heavy French kissing is acceptable moral behavior between an unmarried couple. How many of us parents feel comfortable with this conviction? Consider, too, that a significant minority of young people (36 percent) believe that the fondling of breasts is acceptable moral behavior (with an additional 16 percent uncertain). And note the connection between the designation of certain activities as morally acceptable and the engagement in those activities. This study reveals that the majority of those who believe an action to be acceptable also participate in that action. Our beliefs inevitably guide our actions.

I completed a similar survey with the youth at my church and found the results comparable (though more on the conservative side regarding fondling and premarital sex). In my survey I asked the students to explain why they deemed particular actions as morally acceptable

Our beliefs inevitably guide our actions.

or unacceptable. The majority of my students were unable to provide any explanations. Many simply designated certain actions as moral or immoral based on their own arbitrary convictions. A number of students mentioned Scripture as the basis for determining morality, but when asked why they thought the Bible prohibited premarital sex, they were unable to provide an answer.

SINS OF IGNORANCE

The most disturbing thing about my study, as well as McDowell and Hostetler's study, is not that our children are engaging in immoral sexual behavior. *It's that they don't know that they are doing so!* How can they live lives of sexual purity when they don't know what purity is? Their lack

God has not left us without a knowledge of his will.

of clarity is a testimony to our failure as parents and as pastors. We have not given them an objective, biblical standard by which to judge an action as appropriate or inappropriate. Nor have we explained to them the reasons God prohibits certain activities. We seem to give only subjective biblical standards (Be pure!) and objective personal opinions (Don't French kiss!).

Even when we do offer biblical standards, we aren't able to explain the reason they exist. We can talk of sexual purity all we want, but if we do not know how to define it in objective terms, we do our children (and ourselves) little good. Leaving our children to decide for themselves the definition of purity places on them a burden that God never intended them to bear.

THREE GOD-ORDAINED CATEGORIES

God has not left us without a knowledge of his will. Contrary to what many might believe, God has clearly spelled out what he expects from men and women regarding sexual purity. We will see that God has grouped male/female relationships into three categories. Though the titles I have given to each category may be slightly arbitrary, the categories themselves are not. Each is based on a command that God has given. Different command, different category of relationship.

Understanding these distinct categories is the key to overcoming the subjectivity surrounding sexual purity, helping us to build boundaries of sexual expression.

GOD-ORDAINED CATEGORIES OF MALE/FEMALE RELATIONSHIPS

Family	Neighbor	Marriage
Sexual expression prohibited	Same as Family Relationship	Sexual expression commanded
Leviticus 18:6	1 Timothy 5:1-2	1 Corinthians 7:3–5

THE FAMILY RELATIONSHIP

The first category of God-ordained male/female relationships is the Family Relationship. God's guideline for sexual expression between blood relatives has evolved throughout history. As mentioned earlier, all of God's commands reflect his nature and purposes. This has been true as well for God's commands regarding sexual relations within families. In early Bible times, God did not prohibit sexual relations between blood relatives. But through the Old Testament Law, God changed that standard. "None of you shall approach any blood relative of his to uncover nakedness; I am the LORD" (Leviticus 18:6, NASB).

Today we do not find this command at all unusual or even necessary. The thought of a sexual relationship with someone in our immediate family is revolting to most of us. But this has not always been the case. As we look back through biblical history prior to the Law, we find that sexual relations between blood relatives were not uncommon. Abraham married his half sister (Genesis 20:11, 12). Lot's daughters approached their father while he was drunk and had intercourse with him (Genesis 19:31–36). Jacob married two sisters, a practice later banned under the Law (Genesis 29:23–28). Presumably Cain, Abel, and Seth, as well as Noah's sons, all married blood relatives.

God did not encourage the practice, and we later learn that he disapproved of it (Leviticus 18:26–28). But he did not ban it until the giving of the Law. The reasons for the ban are not clearly detailed, but it appears that sexual relations between blood relatives no longer fit with the new relationship that God had established with his people through the Law.[3] Regardless of the reason for this prohibition, God's command for sexual expression within the immediate family is clear: abstinence. No sexual activity is to occur between blood relatives.

THE MARRIAGE RELATIONSHIP

A second category of God-ordained male/female relationships is the Marriage Relationship. Though God prohibits sexual relations between blood relatives, his command is quite different regarding men and women who are married. Within the context of marriage, sexual relations are not only permissible, they are commanded. In 1 Corinthians 7:3–5 Paul commands married couples *not* to abstain from sexual relations. He writes,

> Let the husband fulfill his duty to his wife, and likewise also the wife to her husband. The wife does not have authority over her own body, but the husband does; and likewise also the husband does not have authority over his own body, but the wife does. Stop depriving one another, except by agreement for a time that you may devote yourselves to prayer, and come together again lest Satan tempt you because of your lack of self-control [NASB].

With the rampant immorality of Paul's day (and ours), it was not good for a husband and wife to withhold sex from one another. But an even deeper reason for a healthy sexual relationship between married couples is seen back in chapter 1. The physical oneness that results from sex between a husband and wife is an image of the spiritual oneness that results from our union with Christ. Sex is a picture of the gospel, and thus our enjoyment of it within the context of this image is necessary. So where God has prohibited sexual relations between blood relatives, he has commanded it in the case of marriage.

THE NEIGHBOR RELATIONSHIP

The last category of male/female relationships is what I have called, for lack of a better term, the Neighbor Relationship. Following Jesus' definition of a neighbor, this category includes all those who are neither a blood relative nor a spouse (e.g., friends, strangers, schoolmates, coworkers). The commands regarding sexual expression for this category are sown throughout the New Testament. In a word, the standard for male/female relationships in this category is purity.

Sexual purity was a significant element in the biblical authors' understanding of holiness, and it is given a good deal of attention in the New Testament. The commands that address the issue of sexual purity can be viewed from both a negative and positive perspective, instructing us about what we are to avoid as well as embrace. From the negative perspective, Scripture warns us that we are to avoid sexual immorality. Consider these examples:

> *We are to embrace a life of righteousness and holiness.*

Romans 13:13—"Let us behave decently, as in the daytime, not in orgies and drunkenness, not in *sexual immorality* and debauchery, not in dissension and jealousy."

1 Corinthians 6:18—"Flee from *sexual immorality.* All other sins a man commits are outside his body, but he who sins sexually sins against his own body."

But Scripture also instructs us from a positive perspective, telling us what we are to embrace. Not only we are to avoid sexual immorality, we are to embrace a life of righteousness and holiness. Note just a couple references:

1 Thessalonians 4:7—"God did not call us to be impure, but to *live a holy life*."

Romans 6:19—"I am speaking in human terms because of the weakness of your flesh. For just as you presented your members as slaves to impurity and to lawlessness, resulting in further lawlessness, *so now present your members as slaves to righteousness, resulting in sanctification* [NASB]."

At its core, the biblical concept of purity is "freedom from defect." When the word "pure" is used to describe the interaction between a man and a woman, the Bible is speaking about a relationship that is free from the defect of sexual immorality. All Christians would agree that sexual immorality should be avoided and sexual purity embraced. The difficulty arises when we try to define exactly what these concepts mean in quantifiable terms. For example, is it adequate to define sexual immorality as simply sexual intercourse between two unmarried people? If so, where does that leave us regarding oral sex between unmarried couples? What about fondling or mutual masturbation?

Many young people in the church today, due to lack of clarity, have limited their concepts of sexual immorality to include only premarital sexual intercourse, leaving open a host of activities that we as parents intuitively believe are inappropriate for our children. But is it merely one person's opinion against another? How do we take a subjective term like "sexual purity" and break it down in a way that is clear and objective?

ABSOLUTE PURITY DEFINED

In light of this confusion, God has provided the clarity we and our children need in 1 Timothy 5:1-2. In this passage Paul does not merely instruct us to be pure; he also links the concept of sexual purity to an objective reality: "Do not rebuke an older man harshly, but exhort him as if he were your father. Treat younger men as brothers, older women as mothers, and younger women as sisters, with absolute purity."[4]

Here Paul is exhorting Timothy as to how he should interact with the various members of his church (i.e., his neighbors). His interaction with the people of his church should be patterned after his relationship with his biological family. But Paul is not instructing Timothy to treat each older man in his congregation as though that man were his literal father in every circumstance

> *God has provided the clarity we and our children need.*

(think of all the Father's Day cards!). Rather he is referring specifically to the way in which Timothy exercises his pastoral authority in their lives, specifically regarding the way he corrects and admonishes an older man. Instead of using his authority toward the older men of his church in a harsh or disrespectful manner, Timothy is to correct them with the same deference and respect he would give his own father. In Paul's day, that idea would have carried a great deal of significance, since culturally one's father was to be treated with the utmost respect. Paul was concerned that Timothy not use his rightful authority to rebuke or correct in a way that would be disrespectful or in conflict with how a young man should treat an older man.

Similarly, when Paul instructs Timothy regarding his pastoral care toward the women of his church, Paul commands him to treat each one as though she were his mother or sister. But the issue of respect and deference is not the main point of this particular analogy. Again Paul is not asking Timothy to treat the women of his church in every circumstance as though each were his literal mother or sister. Rather he has in mind the way Timothy relates to them sexually, which is seen when Paul clarifies his meaning with the phrase "absolute purity." In other words, Timothy's pastoral care in the lives of the women in his church should be carried out with a familial understanding of purity. Paul's use of the word "pure" (*agnos*) in this passage clearly refers to sexual purity. [5]

Just as treating an older man as a father will help ensure against a disrespectful rebuke, so too treating women as mothers and sisters will help maintain a proper sense of purity. And this is the very thing we most desire for our children. Note again Paul's words: "Treat younger men as brothers, older women as mothers, and *younger women as sisters, with absolute purity.*"

By linking the idea of absolute purity with the familial treatment of the opposite sex, we can establish a clear and objective definition of purity regarding our neighbors. Absolute purity then—purity that is totally free of sexual immorality—is synonymous with treating members of the opposite sex as though they were blood relatives.

Paul is not talking to Timothy solely about how he relates to women *as a pastor* but also how he relates to them *as a man*. For Timothy, absolute purity is synonymous with treating the opposite sex as though they were blood relatives. Once the familial treatment of the opposite sex is linked to the concept of purity, this connection is instructive in all situations. It's not as though Timothy is called to absolute purity because he is a pastor and the rest of us are called to mediocre purity. Absolute purity is required of laypeople just as much as pastors. Though the context is dealing with a pastor's relationship to the opposite sex, the application is the same for everyone.

> *Absolute purity is synonymous with treating members of the opposite sex as though they were blood relatives.*

GIVING SUBSTANCE TO SEXUAL PURITY

First Timothy 5:1-2 helps us tremendously in determining what qualifies as sexual immorality. It also gives us an objective standard by which to judge our actions. If a man would not feel comfortable engaging in a particular action with his mother or sister because it would seem sexually inappropriate, then that action is inappropriate for him to do with anyone other than his spouse. (A kiss on the cheek may not be sexual, but a prolonged kiss on the mouth is clearly of a sexual nature.) Anything sexual is to be abstained from while in the Neighbor Relationship and reserved exclusively for the Marriage Relationship. In short, if an activity is inappropriate for a brother and sister, mother and son, or father and daughter, then it is likewise inappropriate for two unwed people.

> *The intent of God's command is to set boundaries, not to erase limitations.*

Keep in mind that the intent of God's command is to set boundaries, not to erase limitations. Many things that would be appropriate for a brother and sister (e.g., sharing a hotel room, traveling across the country together unescorted) would be inappropriate for an unmarried couple. So Paul is not granting license with this injunction but rather is reminding Timothy of the boundaries that would protect his relationships with the opposite sex. He is to do nothing with them sexually that he would not do with his sister or mother.[6]

Confirmation from the Culture

Though acknowledging the connection between sexual purity and family relations, you might think I am making too much of a fuss about the significance of one passage. Though many verses speak about purity in a general, undefined sense, few establish this connection between absolute purity and familial relationships. But when we understand the early church's societal norms regarding sex, we understand why the biblical authors did not typically need to provide an extensive definition of purity. Unlike our present day concept of sex, which tends to be strictly limited to sexual intercourse, the first-century Roman concept was much more holistic.[7]

In New Testament times, the sexual relationship was not broken down into a series of distinguished steps (kissing, caressing, undressing, intercourse), with only the final stage—intercourse—qualifying as "sex." Rather all of these steps were seen as a part of what it meant to "have sex" with another person. Intercourse was merely the consummation of sex, not the sum total of sex. A man and woman who repeatedly initiated and then suddenly cut short their sexual relations (as is common in Christian dating relationships) would have been viewed as a man and woman who repeatedly began to have sex but broke it off before the consummation of the act.

A helpful parallel can be drawn between the biblical understanding of sex and our present understanding of adultery. Technically, adultery can be defined as sexual intercourse between a married individual and someone other than his or her spouse. However, we would never deem as permissible *any* sexual activity (even just light kissing) between such a couple, even if it were to stop short of sexual intercourse. We intuitively understand the concept of adultery to signify not only sexual intercourse but everything that leads up to it. For a married man or woman to enter into a sexual relationship with another person, regardless of whether it concludes in sexual intercourse, is for that person to enter into adultery.

That we often fail to view sex in this manner is seen in how we frequently use the term "physical relationship" to describe the sexual interaction that takes place between Christian dating couples. The use of such a term implicitly suggests the couple's actions are something other than sexual. But kissing is not merely physical—it is sexual. When we frame the issue in these terms, suddenly things begin to move into focus. Asking the age-old question "How far is too far?" in light of this distinction sounds quite different. The question is really asking, "How much of the sex act can I be involved in apart from marriage?" The answer is none. Sex is to be reserved for marriage.

In Paul's day, premarital sexual activity that intentionally stopped short of sexual intercourse for moral reasons would have been strange. Either men and respectable women abstained from it altogether, or men engaged in it fully with prostitutes or mistresses. For a man to initiate a sexual relationship with an upstanding woman outside the context of marriage would have been a grave insult to both her and her family. Such advances were reserved for mistresses and prostitutes (a practice that was so standard for the culture of that day that even Christians at Corinth routinely engaged in such behavior). Further, to begin a sexual relationship with a member of the opposite sex, no matter how minor, was to commit sexual immorality.

> *"Physical relationship" . . . suggests the couple's actions are something other than sexual.*

Given this historical and cultural framework, we can understand why the biblical authors did not feel a need to spell out "how far is too far." It was already understood. We must not allow the biblical authors' silence to cause us to redefine purity in a way that would have been foreign to them. For Paul's readers, the concept automatically meant treating the opposite sex as family. Even apart from an understanding of the cultural and historical norms of the New Testament era, 1 Timothy 5:1-2 makes this connection clear.

THE IMAGE OF GOD PRESERVED

It quickly becomes apparent that the standard of familial purity as established in 1 Timothy 5:2 fits easily with the idea that God ordained sexual intercourse to serve as an image of Christ's relationship to the church. When we remember that God created sex as a means of communicating our supernatural, one-spirit union with the divine life of Christ, we can begin to understand why God expects us to limit its use to the Marriage Relationship. Just as Christ reserves himself exclusively for the church, becoming one-spirit with his Bride, we too are called to reserve our sexuality exclusively for our spouse.

Through sexual activity in general and sexual intercourse in particular, the "one flesh" union of the marriage relationship reflects the reality of our participation "in the divine nature" (2 Peter 1:4). But when our sexuality is expressed outside the context of a permanent marriage relationship (either through premarital sexual relations or adultery), we fail to portray the image of Christ's and the church's exclusive devotion and union to each other.

The restraint required to live out this ideal is great, particularly in a culture that cannot even begin to comprehend the relationship between Christ and his church. But we must always remember for whom our sexuality was made. It was made first for the Lord, intended to be a divine illustration of *his* nature and purposes. To bypass this reality and use it prematurely for our own gratification is to rob it of its significance and meaning, and thus its true pleasure in our own lives. We must not take that which God has created as sacred and use it prematurely in common relationships that fall short of his intention.

> *We must not take that which God has created as sacred and use it prematurely in common relationships that fall short of his intention.*

It is important that we are clear about what absolute purity entails for unmarried men and women: biblically speaking, absolute purity is synonymous with the familial treatment of the opposite sex. Regarding sexual expression, we are to treat our neighbors (anyone who is not a spouse or a blood relative) as though they were our blood relatives. This is the essence of God's external commands regarding absolute purity.

CONCLUSION

God's standards are not arbitrary—and neither is his designation of the distinct types of male/female relationships. Each relationship has a purpose within the image of God, and the guidelines he gives regarding sexual expression within those categories are tied to that image. As we act in accordance with these guidelines, our sexuality bears well the image of God and his divine plan of salvation. Much of the confusion that arises in our children's relationships with the opposite sex stems from their inability to understand and apply the truths of these distinct relationships.

But how is it that we have for so long misunderstood the essence of sexual purity? The standard of purity found in 1 Timothy 5:1-2 is not so complex or lofty that it is impossible to understand. Nor is this standard tucked away in some obscure portion of Scripture. I have, in fact, heard it quoted on many occasions. I believe that part of the reason young people have failed to apply this standard of purity to their dating

> *How is it that we have for so long misunderstood the essence of sexual purity?*

relationships is because they see those situations as distinct from the Neighbor Relationship. Such oversite is unbiblical and has fueled our inability to discern truth in the realm of sexual purity. We cannot invent our own categories of relationships and then remove ourselves from God standards.

DISCUSSION QUESTIONS

What are the three categories of God-ordained male/female relationships?

Who is included in the Neighbor Relationship?

What is God's command regarding sexual purity for the Neighbor Relationship?

How does 1 Timothy 5:1-2 help us objectively define purity?

According to 1 Timothy 5:1-2, how are we to treat members of the opposite sex who are neither our spouse nor our blood relatives?

Chapter 3

THE DATING DILEMMA: PART I

WHY WE HAVE TO ASK, "HOW FAR IS TOO FAR?"

Gerald: So what does it mean, anyway, when you say that you're "going out"?

Student: Well, like, you know, we're dating.

Gerald: Dating? You mean you guys go out on dates together?

Student: It's more than that. I mean, you can go out on dates with someone but not be dating. You know, just going out as friends.

Gerald: Oh. Help me understand. Let's say a guy and a girl are "just friends" and they get together a lot. That doesn't necessarily mean they are "dating," right?

Student: Right.

Gerald: But let's say that the guy decides he likes her as more than a friend. What does he do?

Student: He asks her out.

Gerald: But aren't they already going out?

Student: Well, they're going out on dates, but they're not, you know, *going out,* going out.

Gerald: Oh. So what's the difference between going out as friends and *going out,* going out?

Student: When you're going out as friends, you don't like each other. You're just, you know, friends.

Gerald: You don't like your friends?

Student: Of course you like your friends, but you don't *like them,* like them.

Gerald: I see. You like them, but you don't *like them,* like them.

Student: Now you've got it.

Gerald: Okay. Let's recap. Going out on dates isn't necessarily the same thing as dating. It's dating only when two people like each other—but not just in the friendship kind of like, in the *liking* kind of like.

Student: Yeah, that's about right.

Gerald: So let's say two people like each other as more than just friends, and two other people like each other only as friends. Let's say both couples get together every Friday night and talk on the phone three times a week. What differences might we see between these two relationships that would help us distinguish which is which?

Student: Well, the couple who is going out—

Gerald: You mean *going out,* going out, or just going out?

Student: *Going out,* going out.

Gerald: Gotcha.

Student: Anyway, the couple who is going out might hold hands or something. Or the guy might kiss her.

Gerald: So a difference between a dating couple and a couple who is "just friends" is whether or not they have some sort of physical relationship?

Student: Yeah, I guess so.

Gerald: What if two people who were just friends got together and kissed sometimes? Would that be bad?

Student: Yeah. I mean, they're just friends.

Gerald: But why is it bad for two people who are just friends to kiss each other as long as they're not *really* kissing? What if they just like to kiss for fun?

Student: Well, some of my friends do that, but I don't think it's right. Kissing and stuff is for people who have an official relationship. Otherwise I think it makes it less special—it kind of trivializes it.

Gerald: So you're saying that it would be wrong for two people who were "just friends" to kiss each other just for fun?

Student: Yes.

Gerald: So let's say that you go to a party and you meet this guy there. You don't know each other, but you can tell he likes you and you like him. You take a walk together, and the next thing you know he's trying to kiss you. Is that appropriate?

Student: I wouldn't appreciate it—even if I liked him, I don't think it's right to kiss just anybody.

Gerald: So you're saying that it would be wrong for you to kiss someone you didn't really know that well or had just met?

Student: Yes.

Gerald: So let's say instead that after the party, he starts calling you and you talk on the phone, go out on a few dates, get to know each other, and then he asks you out and makes it official. And then he kisses you good-night. Is that bad?

Student: Then it would be fine, because it would be an official relationship. It's not like you rushed into it or were making out with just anybody.

Gerald: So let's recap. You think it's wrong to kiss your friends just for fun and it's wrong to kiss guys you don't really know that well. Do I have that right?

Student: Right.

Gerald: But you think it's okay to kiss someone whom you're going out with as long as it doesn't get carried away—whatever that means.

Student: Right.

Gerald: So you have a conservative standard of sexual purity regarding how you relate with guys who are "just friends" and with guys you don't know that well, but a more liberal standard regarding guys you are going out with?

Student: Yeah, I guess so.

Gerald: Up until now we've been talking about what you think is right and wrong. But let me ask you a question. Do you think God has a different standard of sexual purity for dating couples than he does for those who are "just friends" or strangers?

Student: Umm ... I guess I never really thought of it like that before.

THE EVOLUTION OF DATING: FROM ACTIVITY TO CATEGORY

The term "dating" has evolved over time to mean something quite different than it used to. In the past, the term "dating" did not describe a category of relationship as much as it described an activity. Unlike previous generations, which understood the term "dating" to be referring to something a guy and girl *did* (e.g., going on a date), the modern concept of dating often refers to something they *are* (boyfriend/girlfriend). In other words, the term is used to distinguish romantic relationships from nonromantic relationships. This shift in meaning is wrought with signifi-cance. As we have come to view dating as a category of relationship separate from nonromantic rela-tionships, we have inadvertently given it the legitimacy that we intuitively give to the three God-or-dained male/ female relationships. Herein lies a potential for great danger, for when we invent our own categories of male/female relationships, we are forced to invent our own purity guidelines within those categories.

> *The term "dating" has evolved over time to mean something quite different than it used to.*

Please observe that my critiques are against dating *relationships,* not against dating. In other words, I am cautioning against dating as a *category of relationship,* not against the activity of going on dates. This is an important distinction that will become clearer as we proceed. In the following diagram, notice how well a dating relationship fits (or rather doesn't fit) with the categories of relationships that God has ordained.

How Dating Fits within the God-Ordained Categories of Relationships

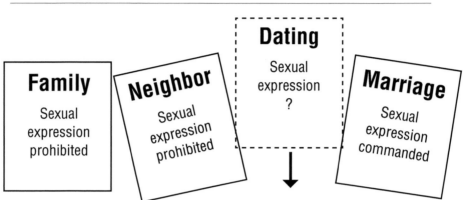

Inventing Our Own Absolutes

The guidelines for sexual expression within the God-ordained categories are clear. But we have created our *own* category, and then wondered at the lack of God's direction as to how we are to behave within that category. Feeling left to our own devices, we have attempted to come up with our own standards of purity in this man-made relationship.

Dating is more than just a Neighbor Relationship, we reason, so surely some level of sexual expression is permitted (at least holding hands, good-night kisses, and snuggling on the couch). Yet it is not quite to the level of the Marriage Relationship, so obviously sexual intercourse is out.

> *We cannot invent our own category of relationship and then make up our own rules.*

The standards of purity for a dating relationship, we conclude, must be somewhere between "just friends" and "just married."

But there is a lot of room between no sexual expression and sexual intercourse! We cannot invent our own category of relationship and then make up our own rules. The reason God does not address the issue of sexual expression within a dating relationship is because he does not recognize a dating relationship as something different than a Neighbor Relationship.

BOUND BY THE NEIGHBOR RELATIONSHIP

As far as God is concerned, all unmarried people are bound to the standards of purity that he has defined in the Neighbor Relationship. This is crucial for our children to realize. Neither we nor our children may invent a new category of male/female relationships and then remove ourselves from God's laws. Regardless of what our children may call another person (boyfriend, girlfriend, etc.), they are still bound by the purity guidelines of the Neighbor Relationship. I cannot stress this point enough. According to God's Word, they are to do nothing with a member of the opposite sex that they wouldn't do with a blood relative. This clarifies things pretty dramatically and gives an objective answer to the question "How far is too far?"

The fact that we even ask this question is an indication that we view a dating relationship as distinct from the Neighbor Relationship. For example, we do not ask this question regarding our sister or cousin. Nor do we typically ask it concerning members of the opposite sex in general. When it comes to those relationships, we intuitively know the answer to the question "How far is too far?" But when we raise the question regarding a dating relationship, we show that we assume a dating relationship to be distinct from these other relationships, the former rules no longer applying. But God's standard for a "dating" couple is the same as God's standard for the Neighbor Relationship. On what basis would we remove ourselves from the standard of familial purity as outlined in 1 Timothy 5:1-2?

THE DATING DECEPTION

As far as God is concerned, dating does not exist as a legitimate category of relationship. Our children don't need to know how to behave in a dating relationship, nor do they just need to abstain from it until they are older. They need to understand that a dating relationship is a shadow relationship, only a parody of the Marriage Relationship.

As parents, we must be very careful that our children do not come to believe that a dating relationship is a real and legitimate form of relationship, free from the guidelines of sexual purity established by God in the Neighbor Relationship. So many of us have been swept up in the lie that God has not spoken in objective standards regarding sexual purity for two people romantically interested in each other. He has. The guidelines for two such people are the same as the guidelines for two people *not* romantically interested in each other: treat one another like blood relatives. Adding the label "dating" to a relationship does not absolve it from these guidelines.

Keeping Things Clear

Many parents feel uncomfortable about the way in which their children interact sexually with their romantic interests. But though they feel uncomfortable, they do not possess any scriptural support for their feelings beyond the idea that such actions could possibly lead to sex. But this argument implies that light sexual interaction is not wrong in itself but only *potentially* wrong in that it *might* lead to sexual intercourse. But scripturally, any sexual expression outside of marriage, regardless of where it leads, is forbidden for the sake of God's image.

As parents, we need to communicate to our children that such actions mar God's purposes for sex. What he intended to be reserved exclusively as a means of conveying Christ's oneness with the church is being used in a relational context that can never convey this image. For the sake of God's image, our children are bound to treat all members of the opposite sex—men, women, young and old—according to the guidelines of the Neighbor Relationship. But even before that, we must help our children see that a dating relationship is not distinct from the Neighbor Relationship. This will help them understand that their relationships with those they are romantically interested in—as far as God's standard of purity is concerned—are

> *Scripturally, any sexual expression outside of marriage, regardless of where it leads, is forbidden for the sake of God's image.*

no different than their relationships with any other people.

Conclusion: The Image of God Undone

Ultimately God has ordained the boundaries of the Neighbor Relationship for the sake of Christ and the church. When our children begin to express themselves sexually (even in minor ways) with someone other than their spouse, they use their sexuality outside of the context for which it was created. God has ordained our sexuality to image forth the relationship between Christ and his church. To break the boundaries established in the Neighbor Relationship causes this image to be blurred and confused.

> *Our sexuality must be reserved exclusively for our spouse, for Christ has reserved himself exclusively for us.*

For the sake of God and his image, our sexuality must be reserved exclusively for our spouse, for Christ has reserved himself exclusively for us. When our children begin to dabble with it in a dating relationship, they rob themselves of the joy of obedience that comes from imaging forth the joy of Christ, and worse yet, distort the image of Christ's pure commitment to his Bride.

DISCUSSION QUESTIONS

What qualifies someone as a boyfriend or girlfriend?

Do you think a boyfriend/girlfriend relationship is different in God's eyes than a Neighbor Relationship?

When it comes to any relationship that does not involve one's spouse, what then is the answer to the question "How far is too far?"

What might be some dangers of placing a title like "dating" or "boyfriend/ girlfriend" on a relationship?

Chapter 4

THE DATING DILEMMA: PART II

PAPER WALLS AND FREE CLIMBING

"It's permanent for now."
—One Hollywood couple's assessment
of their new relationship

What exactly *is* a dating relationship, anyway? I believed in the concept as a young person, but I would not have been able to define it in objective terms. Later, however, as a young adult, I began to wonder if perhaps a dating relationship was nothing more than a mirage, a relationship of smoke and mirrors that appeared to be something other than it was. My conversations with young people have confirmed this suspicion. The previous chapter dealt with the subject of dating from the standpoint of physical and sexual purity. This chapter unpacks the actual logic of dating relationships. As we will see, they remain forever unquantifiable, and any attempt to put flesh and bone to these relationships immediately shows the wispiness of their nature. Perhaps another glimpse into the life of Miss Average Student is in order.

Gerald: I'd like to spend some more time talking about dating relationships if that's okay.

Student: Sure.

Gerald: What is it about an "official" dating relationship that distinguishes it from two people who are just dating and like each other romantically but haven't yet made it official?

Student: Well, in the official relationship, the guy and the girl are committed to each other.

Gerald: What do you mean, "committed?"

Student: Well, you know. It's when two people are committed to dating only each other. It's different than casual dating.

Gerald: What do you mean by casual dating?

Student: Casual dating is when two people are just going out on dates, but they haven't made their relationship exclusive.

Gerald: Exclusive?

Student: Yeah, you know . . . since their relationship isn't exclusive, they can still date other people if they want to.

Gerald: So in casual dating, you can date whomever you want at any time?

Student: That's right.

Gerald: But in an official dating relationship, that's not possible because the two people are committed to each other?

Student: Yeah. It's when they agree that from then on they are going to date only each other.

Gerald: For how long?

Student: Well, it's not forever or anything. Until they get married or until the relationship doesn't work for one or the other.

Gerald: Doesn't work? You mean when one doesn't like the other anymore?

Student: I guess. Or they move or meet someone else or something.

Gerald: So in a committed dating relationship, a guy is free to break up with his girlfriend at any time and date someone else?

Student: Yeah.

Gerald: And casual dating is when you can date anyone you want at any time?

Student: Yeah.

Gerald: So *what's* the difference again?

WOLF IN SHEEP'S CLOTHING: DATING'S PRETENSE OF COMMITMENT

Two people who are "dating" appear in many ways to have a real and established relationship. They have a title for their significant other (boyfriend or girlfriend). They are expected to remember anniversaries, holidays, and birthdays.

They place upon each other certain obligations and restrictions regarding whom they can and cannot spend time with. On the surface there appears to be some real level of commitment. But in

> *Using words like "commitment" when speaking of dating relationships can give a false impression about the reality of such relationships.*

spite of these qualities, the commitment of a dating relationship is really only a veneer. Using words like "commitment" when speaking of dating relationships can give a false impression about the reality of such relationships.

COMMITTED TO WHAT?

I suspect that many dating couples have not really thought through what they mean when they use a word like "commitment" in the context of their relationship. If pressed, however, they usually ascribe the idea of commitment to the fact that they have agreed to date only each other. In other words, a man who is "dating" one woman cannot go out with another at the same time. He is bound to his girlfriend. He has agreed to express his romantic interest in her alone. Thus it is the exclusive nature of the relationship that separates it from other male/female relationships. According to conventional dating practices, a relationship is unofficial until it becomes exclusive.

In short, the transition from friend to boyfriend/girlfriend occurs when the couple agrees to date only each other. On the surface, this does give an impression of commitment. But is the commitment of a dating relationship really a commitment of any substance?

The true nature of commitment in dating can be seen when contrasted with the commitment of a marriage relationship. Unlike a dating relationship, the commitment and exclusivity of marriage is involuntary. As a legitimate male/female relationship, the Marriage Relationship entails certain obligations and responsibilities that are irrevocable. When a man marries his bride, he gives up his right to choose one woman over another. Prior to his marriage, however, his exclusive commitment to his wife was by his own choosing. He had no moral obligation to marry her. But once married, a moral obligation is imposed upon him by the God-given commands of the Marriage Relationship. Morally, he *has* to faithfully love his wife. The die is cast for better or for worse. It is an irrevocable commitment.

> *To our harm, we have tended to give the exclusivity of dating relationships a similar weight as that of marriage.*

To our harm, we have tended to give the exclusivity of dating relationships a similar weight. Though a dating relationship may appear to entail the involuntary exclusivity of marriage, its exclusivity is really no different than that of a casual dating relationship. It can be legitimately dropped at any time by either party. Neither the man nor the woman has any obligation to maintain the exclusivity of a dating relationship. In spite of a dating relationship's apparent commitment, both parties are free to date whomever they choose, whenever they choose. All that the relationship requires is for one to break up with the other prior to doing so.

Unlike divorce in marriage, breaking up is a legitimate part of dating relationships and in no way indicates a breach of honor or commitment. In the end, the apparent involuntary exclusivity of the dating relationship is really only voluntary exclusivity in disguise. Like a house made of paper, dating relationships have the appearance of security and stability, but they lack any true means of achieving it. They are form without function.

The commitment of a dating relationship is simply the commitment to inform the person of one's intention to end his or her commitment before actually doing so. Not much of a commitment! There can be no real promise, no assurance of mutual protection, and no real guarantee for abiding trust. Neither party in a dating relationship has promised anything permanent. I read recently of a Hollywood couple's disturbingly accurate assessment of their new relationship: "It's permanent for now." Inspiring, isn't it?

Free Climbing and the Danger of False Security

My intention is not to point out our misuse of the word "commitment" in dating relationships simply to achieve linguistic accuracy but rather to make us aware of the inherent danger that often accompanies such misuse. Many young people unwittingly depend upon dating relationships as though some measure of real security was truly present in the relationship, and they are susceptible to all sorts of heartbreak when the relationship's temporary nature becomes evident.

When I was first learning to rock climb, my instructor carefully explained all of the safety procedures, emphasizing the supreme importance of the rope, which would act as our security if we were to fall. This rope was carefully attached to my climbing harness and then just as carefully attached to my instructor. Knowing that the rope was present gave me the confidence to climb in ways that I would otherwise not have done. Many times, in fact, I would have fallen and seriously injured myself had the rope not caught me. But though I was very aware of the rope and its presence gave me security, in reality it was not the rope alone that saved me from injury. My true security came from knowing that the rope was anchored securely to an instructor, who had pledged to stay at his post until I had reached the ground safely. The rope itself would have done little good without the commitment of the person who held it.

In many ways, a relationship is like a climber's rope. It is only as secure as that to which it is anchored. Using words like "trust," "security," and "commitment" when speaking of dating relationships can create a sense of security similar to the presence of the climber's rope. But a relationship is only as secure as the commitment to which it is attached.

How foolish it would be for a climber to feel a sense of security from a rope that was not anchored securely. A friend of mine finished a difficult climb only to discover that his rope had been improperly anchored. As he completed his last maneuver, he watched in horror as his anchor pins fell away to the rocks below. Though he felt secure throughout his climb because of the rope's presence, his sense of security was not based on reality. Had he fallen during his climb, he would have been seriously injured or even killed.

In the same way, the "commitment" of a dating relationship often gives the illusion of security. But this commitment is essentially non-existent. Free climbing is a dangerous activity. Free climbing when you only think your safety rope is securely anchored is more dangerous still. This, I believe, is essentially what many dating relationships are: a free climb that has the aura and feel of a guided climb. Consequently, young people are often not fully aware of the danger they face.

THE PARTICULAR VULNERABILITY OF YOUNG WOMEN IN DATING RELATIONSHIPS

Young people often view the exclusivity of a dating relationship as providing a certain measure of security. This can be particularly true regarding young women. Most Christian young women will not enter into a physical relationship with a young man unless he "commits" himself to being her boyfriend (though even this standard is increasingly falling by the wayside). Because of the perception of security in a dating relationship, a woman may give herself away sexually (even when this stops short of intercourse) in ways that she would otherwise hesitate to do with other men that she might be attracted to. But when we understand the true nature of commitment within a dating relationship, we see that this giving of herself is misguided and is based on a false sense of security. Her boyfriend is no more committed to her than any other guy who likes her.

> *A relationship is only as secure as the commitment to which it is attached.*

In many ways, a dating relationship has everything going for the man and nothing for the woman. The man receives a good deal from the woman, but in no way does he have to commit himself to any sort of permanency. The woman gives up the most valuable part of herself only to receive an illusion of security. This false sense of security can lead to heartache. Granted, not all dating relationships end in heartache, but the potential for such pain is increased when the precarious nature of the relationship is not fully realized. As parents, we must help our daughters understand that a man has nothing permanent to offer apart from a marriage proposal. A dating relationship offers no more security than any other relationship.

Betraying a Temporary Commitment?

The confusion resulting from the use of such terms as "commitment" when referring to a dating relationship can be seen in the guilty feelings that often occur during a breakup. Though many dating relationships (especially among young teens) are never taken seriously by either party, many more dating relationships do indeed become intense. The feelings of guilt, anger, and resentment that are so often a part of a breakup should give us a moment of pause.

> *The feelings of guilt, anger, and resentment that are so often a part of a breakup should give us a moment of pause.*

A friend of mind told me of his feelings just prior to ending his relationship with his girlfriend. "I dreaded doing it," he said. "I felt like I was betraying her trust in me." And, in fact, this is how he and his girlfriend both felt when he finally did break up with her. That both would acknowledge the legitimacy of breaking up, yet both feel a sense of betrayal (as though a trust was being broken), indicates that we are often unclear about the nature of commitment within dating relationships. We seem to be unknowingly talking out of both sides of our mouths, using words like "commitment" and "trust" while at the same time acknowledging the freedom to break that commitment and trust at any time.

On the surface, most young people realize *intellectually* that the commitment of a dating relationship is only temporary. But they begin to respond *emotionally* as though the relationship really did entail some measure of permanency, as though the commitment of a dating relationship was somewhere in between the noncommitment of friendship and the total commitment of marriage. But either a couple is committed to one another or they are not. Being temporarily committed is essentially no different than being uncommitted.

Confusing Attraction with Commitment

Ultimately I believe that many young people are confusing attraction with commitment. That two people are attracted to each other today means essentially nothing about how they will feel tomorrow. They have promised nothing to each other about the future. When both parties clearly understand this truth, they will be able to wisely choose how much emotional investment they will make in the relationship. But when we start placing labels on a relationship such as "boyfriend" and "girlfriend" and using words like "commitment," we run the danger of creating a sense that the relationship is built upon something real and solid. But all that really exists is a current mutual attraction. A declaration of attraction is not the basis of security.

> *The insecure nature of dating relationships must not be hidden, for it can lead to misplaced trust and unnecessary heartache.*

A young man I know once insisted to his girlfriend that they drop the labels of boyfriend and girlfriend and restart their relationship within the confines of the Neighbor Relationship. His girlfriend, however, did not like the idea of being classified like any other girl. She greatly resisted the idea and claimed that it would make her feel insecure in his affection toward her. But that was precisely the point! She had no cause for feeling secure in his affections until he proposed. He had made no promises. Any feelings of security that she had in the relationship were built on a sandy foundation of attraction rather than the lasting foundation of commitment.

Conclusion:
It Don't Mean a Thing without the Ring!

Ultimately there is no true security apart from the promise of marriage. This reality is so often masked in dating relationships. Words like "security," "commitment," and "promise" have no place in romantic relationships apart from marriage. It's not that the exclusivity of a dating relationship is illegitimate; rather it simply doesn't exist. Neither party has promised to be exclusive forever, but only for as long as it suits their individual desires. The insecure nature of dating relationships must not be hidden, for it can lead to misplaced trust and unnecessary heartache.

This is why I strongly discourage parents from allowing their children to indiscriminately form "dating" relationships. The temptation to view such relationships as distinct from the guidelines of the Neighbor Relationship will likely be beyond what they are capable of handling. In the end, the real issue is not whether your children have boyfriends or girlfriends. The real issue is whether they understand that regardless of the label they may place on another person, no real commitment or security entitles them the freedom to act outside the guidelines of the Neighbor Relationship.

Because I believe our current system of dating too easily creates an illusion of security, I will suggest in chapter 7 an alternative method to finding a spouse. But before I do, it will be necessary to establish a solid understanding of what God expects regarding romantic purity between an unmarried man and woman.

As we will see in the chapters to come, not only does God place restrictions upon the external *sexual* expression of unmarried men and women, he also places restrictions upon their *romantic* expression as well. Trying to maintain these proper boundaries in a "dating relationship" is nearly impossible. Everything about such relationships is focused on fanning into flame precisely what God has intended us to reserve until marriage.

Discussion Questions

Is it fair to say that a boyfriend and girlfriend are committed to each other? If so, in what way?

What is the difference between commitment in marriage and commitment in a dating relationship?

Two follow-up questions that may help illustrate this point are:

Can a guy legitimately break up with his girlfriend and date another woman?

Can a married man legitimately break up with his wife and date another woman?

Why might it be dangerous to use a term like "commitment" regarding a dating relationship?

Is it any safer for a girl to give herself away sexually to a guy because he is her boyfriend?

Chapter 5

THE HEART OF THE MATTER

UNDERSTANDING THE BIBLICAL PERSPECTIVE ON LUST

"You have heard that it was said, 'Do not commit adultery.' But I tell you that anyone who looks at a woman lustfully has already committed adultery with her in his heart."

—Jesus

Hopefully it is becoming clear that we must formulate a new method of spouse finding. But before we attempt to do so, a word still needs to be said regarding the appropriate timing and context for the release of sexual desire. Are we to simply keep our children from forming dating relationships but otherwise allow them to desire from afar? A sort of "love but don't touch" kind of methodology? Has God given us any direction regarding sexual desire? He has, but we have often misunderstood Scripture's depiction of lust, as well as its antidote. We need to get back to the heart of the matter.

Scripture tells us that sexual desire is controllable and is not to be released toward just anyone, a concept that is in direct contrast to our culture. As we will see, God asks us not only to control our sexual *activity* but our sexual *desire* as well, arousing it only with our future spouse. This guideline also flows directly from the fact that God has created the sexual relationship between a man and a woman as a type of Christ's relationship with the church.

Understanding the Nature of Lust: A Key to Emotional Purity

Does sexual desire originate from our bodies or our hearts? Can it be controlled, and if so, how? Is sexual desire different from lust? If sexual desire is good because it is from God, when does it become lust?

When our children correctly understand the characteristics of

> *Sins of the heart are just as destructive to God's image as sins of the flesh.*

lust, as well as how to control it, they will have a proper foundation upon which to build a life of sexual purity. Ultimately they need to understand that sexual desire is first emotional before it is mental or physical, and that sins of the heart are just as destructive to God's image as sins of the flesh.

Matthew 5:27: In His Heart . . .

As we begin to explore this issue, let's look first at Matthew 5:27-28. This passage will provide the foundation for all we say in this chapter about lust.

> You have heard that it was said, "Do not commit adultery." But I tell you that anyone who looks at a woman lustfully has already committed adultery with her in his heart.

The Greek word translated "lustfully" in this passage is the word *epithumeo* and is often translated in our English Bibles as simply "to desire" in a positive sense or "to lust" and "covet" in a negative sense. The same word was used for both. Consider these examples of how the biblical authors used this same word in a positive context:

Matthew 13:17—"For I tell you the truth, many prophets and righteous men longed [*epithumeo*] to see what you see but did not see it, and to hear what you hear but did not hear it."

Luke 22:15—"And he said to them, 'I have eagerly desired [*epithumeo*] to eat this Passover with you before I suffer.'"

The Neutrality of Desire

In these two passages, *epithumeo* is translated in a positive sense, even in reference to Christ and the prophets. So the same biblical word describes the holy longing that Christ and the prophets had for the things of God and also the sinful longing that a man can have for a woman other than his wife. What is the point? Simply this: desire itself, from a biblical perspective, is amoral. It is neither right nor wrong. It's like shooting a gun—it all depends on what you're shooting at. Look again at our first passage. It could easily be translated in this way: "I tell you that anyone who looks at a woman *with desire for her* has already committed adultery with her in his heart." So when Christ instructs us not to "lust" after another woman, he is simply telling us not to "desire" another woman.[1] He is essentially affirming the Old Testament Law, " 'You shall not covet [*epithumeo*, or desire] your neighbor's wife' " (Deuteronomy 5:21).

Both legitimate and illegitimate sexual desire can feel the same. The intense sexual arousal that a man feels toward his wife may be little different than the sexual arousal that a man feels toward his mistress. Though there is little difference in the sexual feelings themselves, in the former case his desires are pure, and in the latter they are sinful. It is not wrong to desire a sexual relationship with one's wife or to desire a sexual relationship in general. (We must not give our children the impression that they should not have sexual desire—this is both impossible and unbiblical.) Both of these desires have legitimate objects as their goal. But when we direct that sexual desire toward someone other than our spouse, we have moved into sin, for now we desire something that is not ours to possess.

> *What makes desire sinful is the object of that desire, not the desire itself.*

The Proper Object of Desire

Suppose my neighbor comes home with a unique handmade rug from China and invites me over to see it. This rug could excite within me both legitimate and illegitimate desire. If, when looking at his rug, I am filled with jealous desire for his rug (even though he has no intention of ever selling it), then that is sinful desire, for the rug is his to possess and not mine. But if upon seeing his rug I am happy for him and filled with a desire to go out and buy a unique rug of my own, then my desire is pure. This is what the Law was getting at when the Israelites were told not to covet (*epithumeo*, or desire) their neighbors' servants, donkeys, and oxen. It was not wrong for Israelites to desire donkeys or servants of their own. But when they jealously desired to possess what someone else had already laid proper claim to, they sinned.

An important principle can be gleaned from Christ's words.

> *It is not enough that our actions align with the Word of God. Our hearts must do so as well.*

Though we often tend to define sin as an act of the body, Christ reveals that the desire to commit a sin is itself a sin. It is not enough that our actions align with the Word of God. Our hearts must do so as well. Just because I do not actually strike my brother when I greatly desire to strike him does not mean that I am free from sin. The man who refrains from murder but hates his brother in his heart is guilty of murder (Matthew 5:21, 22). In the same way, the man who desires to commit adultery yet refrains is still guilty of adultery in his heart.

Better, of course, to refrain from sinful desire than to give in to it, but better still not to desire sin at all. This is the sum total of Christ's sermon and the manner in which he defines true righteousness: we must not only choose the right, we must desire the right.

Most importantly, our children must understand that Christ's command against lust does not apply to married men and women alone. When out with a few of my single friends, someone commented about an attractive young woman passing by. One of my friends poked me in the ribs and commented, "You can't be looking anymore now that you're married." It was as though I had a prohibition against lust because I was married, but since they were not, desiring this woman was acceptable for them.

Such a perspective misses the whole point of Christ's commands and reveals a limited understanding of lust. Christ did not address his comments about lust simply to married men and women. The young man who looks with lust upon a young woman who is not his wife desires something that is not his to possess. Since she is not his wife, he has no right to use her as a means of arousing his sexual passions. Just as it is wrong for a young man to engage in sexual activity with a young woman who is not his wife, so too it is wrong for him to *desire* to engage in sexual activity with that young woman.

The prohibition against lust is not for the sake of the spouse but rather for the sake of sexual purity itself as it relates to the image of God, specifically Christ and the church. When we direct our sexual desire toward someone other than our spouse (whether we are married or not), we use our sexuality in a way that is inconsistent with Christ's single-minded commitment and devotion to his church. The only time it is permissible to arouse our sexual desire toward another person is when that person is our husband or wife.

LUST IN THE HEART, NOT THE MIND

In understanding the biblical view of lust, we must also be mindful of its location. Too often we confuse exactly where lust takes place. Look again at the words of Christ in Matthew 5:28 and notice the location of lust: " 'Anyone who looks at a woman lustfully has already committed adultery with her *in his heart.*' "

Lust does not take place in the mind but in the heart. This makes sense, of course, when we understand that the term "lust" is simply another word for "desire." Many people have a misperception that lust involves some sort of sexual fantasy or an exercise of the mind. A man must "undress her in his mind," so to speak. But according to Christ's own words, lust takes place in the heart, not the mind, and a person can lust without allowing him or herself to succumb to a sexual fantasy.

The indiscriminate rush of sexual desire and excitement that we feel for an individual of the opposite sex is precisely the thing that Christ is referring to. This truth is very convicting. Even the unregenerate can control their thoughts. This does not require the power of

> *Lust does not take place in the mind but in the heart.*

the Holy Spirit any more than abstaining from adultery does. But only a Christian can have a heart ruled by God that desires only what it should. Let us be very clear about what Christ is saying. Just because a person does not allow himself to delve into sexual fantasies about the opposite sex does not in any way mean that he is free from lust. To lust is simply to desire something that should not be desired. Anytime someone other than our spouse arouses within us a desire for that person, we have moved into the sin of lust.

Who Controls Desire?

Many commentators attempt to soften the strictness of Matthew 5:27-28 by contending that it is our *intention in looking* (looking at a woman with the intention of arousing sexual desire) rather than our desires themselves that Christ is condemning (following the NAS and KJV). Thus they contend that Christ in this context is not condemning *inadvertent* sexual desire, which "spontaneously" arises upon seeing an attractive member of the opposite sex.

This interpretation, in my mind, is neither required by the Greek text (see the NIV and RSV) nor is it in keeping with the spirit of the passage.[2] Such commentators seem to imply that as long as we are not looking at another person with the intention of lusting after him or her, it doesn't count as lust even if we do end up lusting. But Christ's whole point in the Sermon on the Mount (of which this command is a part) is that our *desire* to commit sin (in this case, desiring a sexual relationship with someone other than our spouse), not just the actual carrying out of that desire, constitutes sin.

Rage, hatred, and condemnation—just like sexual desire—also seem to well up spontaneously, particularly when we are suddenly confronted with difficult circumstances. Yet nowhere in the Sermon on the Mount does Christ excuse these emotional responses because they are not premeditated or solicited. Rather he condemns them (Matthew 5:22). Spontaneous emotional responses are not morally neutral; they reveal the conditions of our hearts. When we spontaneously respond in rage to the rude driver, in condemnation to the fallen saint, or in lust to the attractive woman, we reveal that the agendas of our hearts are not as aligned with God as they should be.

Let us not deceive ourselves. If we spontaneously desire a member of the opposite sex, we have entered into the realm of lust, even if we don't continue to cultivate that desire or follow through with it. We are, in that moment, desiring that which is illegitimate. Better to overcome lust than to give in to it, but better still not to lust at all.

The more liberal interpretations of Matthew 5:27-28 are in keeping with an age that increasingly views sexual desire as an appetite of the body, as uncontrollable as hunger and thirst. Even we Christians have fallen into this misperception. We must not define sexual arousal as strictly an act of the body rather than a passion of the heart. This is clearly not the biblical perspective. It is true that no amount of commands from our will can make our body cease to feel hunger, thirst, or pain. But sexual desire is more than just a bodily appetite. The fact that we are told to control it is a clear indication that we can, in fact, control it (see Song of Songs 2:7). Christ's commands would be essentially meaningless if this were not the case.

Our sexual desire is the place where our bodies and souls unite. Its desires are felt in both the material and immaterial parts of who we are. But though sexual desire is felt in the body, its command center is in our will, our person. *We,* not our bodies, are in control of our sexual desire. When I

> *We, not our bodies, are in control of our sexual desire.*

speak of controlling desire, I do not simply mean not acting upon one's desires but rather actually choosing that which one desires. But I fear many of us Christians have forgotten this fundamental truth. We readily affirm that a person can control his or her sexual activity, but we do not always affirm the idea that a person can control sexual desire.

Author Dannah Gresh, for example, though providing a great deal of helpful insight in the arena of sexual purity, mistakenly contends that sexual arousal is the result of a chemical reaction in the body and thus is uncontrollable. She states,

> Many of our bodies' responses are activated by the autonomic nervous system (ANS). This system is not controlled by the will, but by the environment. Ever been in a fender-bender? Remember that sick feeling in your stomach and the rapid pulse? You felt physically different because of the environmental change. You cannot control these reactions by choice. The ANS forces the body to respond to the environment.
>
> Sexual arousal works the same way. Things in the environment—what we see, what we hear, and what we

smell—create sexual response. This is particularly strong in a man since God created him to be visually stimulated. If he sees a woman walk by wearing revealing clothing, what happens in his body? He may notice the change in his pulse, his body temperature will rise and blood begins to pump rapidly through his body.... While a man can choose how to respond to this arousal, he cannot control that it has occurred.[3]

I can speak from personal experience that such a view is simply not accurate. Though Gresh is correct about the biological factors of sexual arousal, she sources it incorrectly. Contrary to Gresh's conclusion, the autonomic nervous system (ANS) is not controlled by our environment but by our *perception* of the environment's effect on our well-being. The difference is significant. In a fender bender, it is not the accident itself that causes the ANS to respond but our *perception* that the pending accident could potentially threaten our well-being. When we perceive that the situation we are facing is dangerous, our bodies respond accordingly.

Let us consider a similar situation. I am riding in a vehicle driven by a professional stunt driver. I hang on for dear life as the car careens around a twisty racetrack at speeds that I never even thought were possible. As a first-time passenger, I am not convinced of the driver's ability to avoid a crash, thus my perception of the event as dangerous to my well-being causes my ANS to dump adrenaline into my system. My pulse quickens, my breathing gets shorter, my stomach churns.

But the stunt driver, on the other hand, has driven this particular track so many times that he could do it in his sleep. Quite different than mine, his perception of the same environment has a far different effect. His body does not respond with the same adrenaline rush, for he does not perceive the environment as threatening to his well-being.

If I were to safely ride with the stunt driver many more times on this same circuit, my ANS would respond quite differently than it did the first time, for I would no longer perceive the ride as threatening to my well-being. Thus it is not my environment (a wild car ride) that triggers my ANS but my *perception* of the environment's effect on my well-being.

Ultimately our ANS is triggered based upon the convictions that we hold regarding all of life. It is because we firmly believe that guns, car wrecks, terminal illnesses, and growling dogs are all detrimental to our well-being that our ANS responds when we face those situations.

Our bodies respond automatically to our perception of not only negative environments but also to positive environments. This is seen in the body's response to sexual stimuli. But it is not the environment (scantily clad men or women, billboards, etc.) that triggers our ANS, but rather our perception that the object is extremely beneficial to our well-being.

That sexual arousal is triggered by our perception of an object rather than the object itself is seen in the decline of sexual desire when a sexual relationship has gone sour. Upon first sight of his

> *Our bodies respond automatically to our perception of not only negative environments but also to positive environments.*

mistress, a married man is extremely aroused. Wrongly, he perceives her as the absolute best thing for his well-being. Just the sight of her causes his pulse to quicken and his body to respond in sexual arousal. But as the relationship progresses, he finds that she is not who he thought she was. Before long she is blackmailing him, threatening to make their relationship known unless he pays her off. Now suddenly the man no longer sees her as beneficial to his well-being. The very thought (let alone the sight) of her causes him to be sick to his stomach. He can't even imagine being sexually attracted to her. He hates her with a passion.

In this case, the same stimulus has two very different effects on the man based upon his perception of how it will affect his well-being. This transition from sexual desire to hatred is illustrated in the Bible as well. David's son Amnon followed an almost identical path when his sexual desire for his half sister Tamar turned into intense disgust (see 2 Samuel 13:1–17). So in the realm of sexual arousal, it is not the environment but our perception of the environment's benefit to our well-being that triggers ANS.

SEXUAL SATISFACTION AND THE PEACE OF GOD

Augustine taught that our hearts are restless until they find rest in God alone. Our ANS is triggered so readily by the opposite sex, because nothing else in life so naturally seems to satiate the deep sense of restlessness that lurks within the human heart. As creatures that exist in the image of God, nothing comes closer to the genuine, all-satisfying experience of God than an intimate relationship with one who exists in that image. It is this same idea that caused one person to say that a man knocking on the door of a brothel is a man looking for God. Nothing comes closer to satisfying our restless need for spiritual union with God than does the physical union of the sexual relationship.

When we fail to realize that true satisfaction can be found only in God, we often bounce from one sexual/romantic relationship to another, incorrectly assuming that the lack of satisfaction and sexual arousal we are feeling in the current relationship will be achieved in the next. Each new relationship, then, begins with the promise of ultimate satisfaction, and the ANS responds accordingly. But as the new relationship progresses, the promise of deep fulfillment is not met and we no longer perceive it as beneficial for our well-being. Thus our ANS does not trigger sexual arousal with the same intensity.

> *Our hearts are restless until they find rest in God alone.*

In each case the stimulus (the sexual relationship) does not change; what has changed is our perception of the relationship's ability to meet our deepest needs.[4]

Believing the Truth about Sexual Immorality

When we are firmly convinced that sexual immorality is harmful to our well-being, it looses its grip on us and does not awaken within us sexual desire. Though we are fallen people for whom such conviction comes with great difficulty, it can indeed come. Such conviction takes great faith, but it grows as we embrace the unseen reality of Christ above and beyond what seems so immediately satisfying. We must by faith grasp firmly, and with deep conviction, the truths of God.

Do we really believe that the path of the adulteress leads to death (Proverbs 7:10, 27), that God will judge the sexually immoral who do not repent (Hebrews 13:4; Revelation 21:8), and that no sexual satisfaction exists apart from living out the image of Christ's union to his Bride? Our ANS will be the indicator. We will never become convinced of the truth of Christ until we are deeply united to the person of Christ. We must know Christ himself, his heart, his character, before we can have faith in his commands. We must not just *believe* that his ways are best; we must *know* that his ways are best. Such knowledge comes through our personal experience with Christ himself. And such experience comes from our deep spiritual union with him via his Holy Spirit.

Ultimately, as we participate in the unseen reality of Christ, experiencing his very presence in our lives day to day, we grow in our convictions that his claims are in fact true, that his ways are indeed the best ways, and that nothing can satisfy apart from him.

Do we believe it is possible for a man to see a beautiful woman, perhaps who is dressed inappropriately, perhaps even attempting to seduce him, yet not desire her in his heart or be sexually aroused? Are we merely victims of our circumstances, needing to hide from the world lest we encounter anything that would force us to lust?

Our children must be firmly convinced that it is indeed possible to control and harness their desires, not merely their actions. To be sure, sexual desire is not controlled in the same manner that we control our arms and legs. More than just a mere decision of the will is required. But we do control our sexual desire indirectly through what we believe about the reality of Christ, sexual immorality, and the truth of God. As we become absolutely convinced in our hearts and souls that God's ways are indeed the best ways, we will master our sexual desire.

> *We will never become convinced of the truth of Christ until we are deeply united to the person of Christ.*

Our bodies respond only in accordance with our convictions, and how we spontaneously react to life's circumstances will reveal what we believe. Just as it is possible to become a more spontaneously patient driver and a more instinctively gracious believer in Christ, so too it is possible to become more reflexively pure in our inadvertent encounters with the opposite sex. With the core belief that sexual desire is ultimately in their control, our children *can* build a life of inward purity.

CONCLUSION

It is important to understand what makes desire sinful. Following the biblical use of this word, a definition of "lust" (or "sinful desire") would be "to desire something that is not ours to possess." This has significant application regarding both the sexual and romantic aspects of our sexuality. Anytime we desire something that is not ours to possess, we are sinning.

In the next chapter we will see that God has instructed us to control our romantic desire, as well, until it can be properly expressed within the context of marriage.

Though you may be in full agreement up to this point, you might be wondering about the practicality of this perspective when it comes to your child trying to find a spouse. "Am I really supposed to tell my children," you might be wondering, "that they are not to desire the opposite sex? How do they pick a spouse then?" Good questions! But rather than answering them now, let's save them for the next chapter.

DISCUSSION QUESTIONS

Read Matthew 5:27-28. Explain to your children that the word "lust" simply means "to desire." It may be helpful to read Matthew 13:17 and Luke 22:15 as well.

What makes some desires sinful and some pure? (Help your children see that anytime they desire something that they should not desire, they are sinning.)

When is desire for a man or woman sinful?

When is desire for a man or woman not sinful?

Chapter 6

FALLING IN LOVE ONCE
TEACHING YOUR CHILDREN TO GUARD THEIR HEARTS

"Do not arouse or awaken love until it so desires."
—The Bride of Solomon

In the previous chapter we discussed God's standard for sexual purity. In this chapter we will explore God's standard for romantic purity. As we will see, God has not left us to ourselves to set the boundaries of romantic purity. Like God's commands governing physical relationships, his commands regarding romantic purity also relate to the image of God.

> *Ultimately we are to fall in love only once.*

Following these commands not only enables our young people to use their sexuality in a way that honors God but also provides them the freedom and security that comes from living out God's ideal.

Ultimately we are to fall in love only once. This is God's ideal for male/female relationships. Christ reserves his love and affection for his Bride, and the church is to reserve its love and affection for Christ. Neither one "dates around," giving their hearts away indiscriminately. We, as Christians, have communicated the need to abstain from premarital sex and lust, but we have spoken little of the need to abstain from premarital romance. That's what this chapter addresses. As we will see, Scripture teaches that we are to help our children guard their hearts, not awakening romantic love until it can be expressed within the permanent confines of marriage.

LESSONS FROM THE SONG: SONG OF SONGS 2:3-7

Song of Songs is a statement about the beauty and worth of sexual love and romance. In this short and sensual book, Solomon unabashedly exalts the glory of the sexual relationship between a man and his wife. Though much of the imagery in the book is foreign to the modern reader, we are able to immediately discern important truths about the appropriate timing and context for the release of sexual and romantic desire. Note the passionate language with which Solomon's bride describes her desire for her husband:

> Like an apple tree among the trees of the forest is my lover among the young men. I delight to sit in his shade, and his fruit is sweet to my taste. He has taken me to the banquet hall, and his banner over me is love. Strengthen me with raisins, refresh me with apples, for I am faint with love. His left arm is under my head, and his right arm embraces me (Song of Songs 2:3-6).

The context of this passage focuses on the bride and the consummation of her relationship with Solomon. Apparently on the eve of her wedding, she describes herself as "faint with love" to the point that she needs to be refreshed with food. She is clearly swooning and delighting to do so. But in the

> *"Do not arouse or awaken love until it so desires."*

midst of this enamored, love-sick state, she is mindful of the young maidens who are attending her. She gives them the following charge: "Daughters of Jerusalem, I charge you by the gazelles and by the does of the field: Do not arouse or awaken love until it so desires" (2:7).[1]

Fearing that the arousal of her passions would likewise arouse the passions of the young women around her, Solomon's bride exhorts them not to arouse or awaken their sexual/romantic passions until "love so desires." This charge has two important elements.

Arousing Love

The first element is the charge not to "arouse or awaken love." There is an honesty in this phrase that is refreshing. Solomon's bride acknowledges that within the hearts of young women (and likewise young men) is a desire for love, sex, and romance. Her charge is not to deny this desire but rather to refrain from stirring it up. The picture is much like that of a fire that has been allowed to burn down to a bed of hot coals. Within the coals is the potential for a raging fire, given the proper "stirring up." This is precisely what young unmarried people are not supposed to do. It is no use to tell our kids that they should not have sexual desire. God has placed it within their hearts, and its absence would be an indication of something gone wrong rather than an indication of righteousness. Nevertheless, we are told to refrain from arousing or awakening it outside of its proper context. Thinking back to our understanding of lust, God is asking us to refrain from focusing our sexual desire on a specific person or object that is not our spouse.

> *We are not to stir up romantic love in our hearts outside a marriage relationship.*

Until Love Desires

The second element of this charge addresses the issue of timing. Solomon's bride exhorts the young maidens to refrain from arousing or awakening love "until it so desires." Within the context of this passage, this phrase explains the proper timing for when we are permitted to awaken love. In other words, it could be paraphrased, "until the time is right" or more specifically, "until love can be rightly expressed in marriage." Solomon's bride is not simply saying, "Don't arouse love until you feel like it." The release from this charge is when love, not the person, desires. Love is personified in this passage as the guardian and keeper of itself. When love grants permission, then a person may arouse sexual desire. And within the context of this passage, clearly sexual desire is to be aroused within the context of the marriage relationship.

Love has obviously granted permission to Solomon's bride to arouse and awaken itself, for she has approached a place in life in which erotic, romantic love can be rightly expressed. But as for the young maidens, love does not desire to be aroused, for there is no legitimate outlet for its expression. Ultimately then, we are not to stir up romantic love in our hearts outside the context of a marriage relationship. This has obvious implications for young men and women in their early adolescent years. We must help our children understand that they are to refrain from doing things that cause them to arouse romantic love in their hearts prior to its ability to be properly consummated in a marriage relationship.

In a culture that constantly attempts to prematurely stir up romantic, erotic love, this admonition is difficult to live by. But it is so important that we and our children realize that God asks us to refrain from stirring up and casting romantic desires upon those who are not our betrothed. Ultimately

> *We often think that young women tend to be freer from lust than young men.*

this command makes a great deal of sense in light of the image of God that is expressed through the sexual/romantic relationship. God has created the sexual relationship, romantic desire included, to serve as a type of Christ's supernatural relationship with the church (Ephesians 5:22–32). Just as Christ reserves his affections for his bride, so too we are to reserve our affections for our future spouse. When we place our romantic affections upon a person who is not our life partner, we use those desires in a way that is inconsistent with the image of God.

WOMEN AND EMOTIONAL LUST

The issue of emotional lust will perhaps have most application to our daughters. Women in general, particularly young women, often do not have a strong desire for sexual intercourse per se. What they long for is not the sex act but rather the feelings of security, romance, and affection that accompany a physical relationship. Because they do not desire sex as an end in and of itself, we often think that young women tend to be freer from lust than young men.

But Christ's command is not merely against desiring sex with a particular person but rather against desiring a person in any capacity that should be reserved for marriage. So though a woman may desire only romantic affection from a particular man, this is no less the sin of lust than a man who desires sex from a woman. She desires something from the man that is not hers to possess: his romantic affections. Those affections are to be given to his betrothed alone and must not be separated from marriage. For a woman to seek romantic affection from a man who is not her husband is to seek to stir up love in her heart in ways that God has forbidden.

IS THIS PRACTICAL?

Now back to the questions you may have been asking earlier. If our children are not to allow themselves to desire anyone other than their spouse, how do they choose a spouse they don't desire?

First, we must keep in mind that desire is neutral and that it is the object of the desire that makes a desire sinful. Therefore, it is not wrong for an unmarried man to desire to know a woman sexually *in the future* as his wife. It is wrong only when he desires to know her sexually *in the present,* regardless of whether she is his wife. Let me illustrate:

Stan spies Betty across the room. He knows a little about her, and what he knows he likes very much—including the way she looks. He is at the point in life where he is looking for a wife and is interested in the possibility that she be that wife. Included within the desire to make her his wife is the legitimate desire to know her sexually as his wife. But since Stan is a

> *We must keep in mind that it is the object of the desire that makes a desire sinful.*

righteous man, he has no desire to profane Betty's honor (or God's) by entering into a sexual relationship with her outside marriage.

Imagine that Stan's friend, noticing Stan's interest in Betty, asks, "Hey, do you want to take Betty to a hotel room and have sex with her tonight?" Stan replies, "Absolutely not! In no way do I desire to dishonor Betty in that way." Though he finds her sexually desirable, he places that desire within the context of marriage and, therefore, the thing that he desires (a sexual relationship within marriage) is legitimate. Thus his desire is not sinful. But if Stan were to spy Betty across the room and desire to know her sexually regardless of whether or not they were married, then his desire would be sinful.

If they are honest with themselves, the vast majority of young people have sexual desires that are not within their proper contexts.

Sixteen-year-old boys do not go to the pool to look for wives, nor when they see a girl sunning herself do they say, "Boy, I really would like to marry that girl." Until a person is ready for marriage and actively looking for a spouse, there is little hope that the individual is directing his or her sexual desire toward a person in a pure way.

The same holds true for romantic desire. Just as a man may desire to know a woman sexually within the context of marriage and still be pure, a woman may desire to know a man romantically within the context of marriage and still be pure. Women have (or should have) a certain reservation when they begin to sense a growing attraction to a man. Even in our present dating culture, many non-Christian women refrain from immediately throwing themselves emotionally at a man the moment he shows interest in her. She maintains a wall, waiting until he declares himself. Only then does she begin to open up emotionally and depend on him for romance and affection.

Be content to wait until "love so desires."

What I am arguing for here is that this moment of surrender should happen at marriage (or engagement, as we will discuss later), rather than at some subjective point in a dating relationship. So just like a person can desire sex within the context of marriage, a person can desire romance and affection within the context of marriage.

It is not wrong for your son or daughter to desire the sexual/romantic relationship that will come from marriage, but he or she must be content to wait until "love so desires" before arousing or awakening it—in other words, until such time as those desires may be acted upon. So the real question your children must ask themselves is, "Do I desire this person sexually and romantically now, regardless of marriage? Or am I content to wait until my desire for this person can be properly aroused and expressed within the context of marriage?"

Like all commands in Scripture, the need for romantic purity relates back to the image of God. To give your heart away (though you keep your body) prior to marriage is to paint a picture of a Christ and church that give their affections to someone other than one another. From the beginning of time, Christ has reserved his deepest affections and desires for the church, even before he met her. And from the earliest days of creation, the righteous saints have waited with monogamous longing for the coming of the Promised One. This image must be expressed within our children's own wait for marriage. Christ was faithful in body and heart to a bride whom he had not yet met. He desired none but the one whom God had given him, and, likewise, our children are called to the same faithfulness.

ENGAGEMENT AND THE BRIDE OF CHRIST

I have been talking about suppressing romantic desire until marriage, but in keeping with the image of Christ and the church, I see legitimacy in allowing these desires during engagement. In a very real sense, we Christians are currently engaged to Christ. Though the full consummation of our union with our heavenly bridegroom has not yet occurred,[2] during this "spiritual engagement" our hearts are turned toward him and we long for his return. Our emotional dependency on Christ is legitimate, because our pending wedding with him is as sure as his promise. It *will* come to pass. Thus, it is proper for us to give our hearts away to him during this engagement period.

Likewise, it would seem appropriate to release sexual/romantic desire toward our future spouse, beginning to arouse and awaken romantic love once the certainty of marriage is achieved. This still means, however, that the desire we awaken must seek its fulfillment within the context of marriage, not before. But it does allow for two people to begin stirring up the coals of romantic desire in preparation for their wedding day. This freedom, however, presupposes a biblical understanding of engagement.

In biblical times, an engagement resembled a business transaction more than anything else. It was a legally binding affair, not to be entered into lightly; in fact, a divorce was necessary in order to break it (see, for example, the account of Joseph and Mary). Though in our culture, engagement is not a *legally* binding affair, it is nonetheless in God's eyes a *morally* binding affair. The pledge to marry is a pledge of one's word. Unlike the commitment of a dating relationship, the commitment of an engagement is real and solid. Both the man and the woman

> *It seems that for many in today's culture, engagement is seen as a trial period, not binding on either party.*

have offered a real promise of permanent substance. It is not merely a declaration of affection but a declaration of lifelong commitment. Giving one's heart away to his fiancée assumes that he will stand by his word.

Sadly, however, it seems that for many in today's culture, engagement is seen as a trial period, not binding on either party. We must teach our children not to give their word lightly and without a great deal of thought and prayer. Though perhaps it would be better to break off an ill-thought-through engagement rather than proceed into a bad marriage, I still believe that this would be only the lesser of two evils. We must

> *Christ fell in love once; we fall in love once.*

let our yes be yes and our no be no. To break our word is a sin. We must advise our children so they do not put themselves in a position where they would have to choose between the sin of breaking their word and the sin of following through with a marriage that God has not blessed.

CONCLUSION

In view of the issue of sexual/romantic purity, a dating relationship has much potential for harm. The whole point of the dating relationship is to experience some (if not all) of the initial elements of love and romance. Few will be able to maintain the scriptural bounds of physical purity, and fewer still will be successful at fulfilling God's commands regarding emotional purity.

Both the sexual and emotional desires of our children, though they must not be denied, must not be fanned into flame until a proper context arises in which to express those desires. For the sake of God's image, that context is marriage. Christ fell in love with only the church, and likewise the church reserves its affection for Christ. Our romantic affections are to be patterned after this reality. Christ fell in love once; we fall in love once.

At this point, many of you, as parents, may be agreeing with me but are having a difficult time envisioning where one could possibly go from here. We have shed our old garments, so to speak, but we haven't yet discovered our new ones. That's what the next chapter is about.

Discussion Questions

According to Song of Songs 2:3–7, when is the proper time to arouse and awaken our desire for someone?

What are ways that we might inappropriately arouse or awaken love? (A couple responses, for example, are by dating or too much daydreaming.)

Why does God command us to refrain from arousing our romantic and sexual passions until we are married? (Help your children connect this command to the image of Christ and the church and the romantic purity that both expressed as they waited for one another.)

Chapter 7

FRIENDSHIP: THE "NON-APPROACH" APPROACH

SWITCHING CATEGORIES WITHOUT CREATING NEW ONES

Jennifer reached across the table and closed Tom's menu. "They come quicker when they know you're done looking at the menu," she said.

Tom laughed. "Who are you who are so wise in the ways of ordering?"

Jennifer smiled. "I have many secrets."

"Speaking of secrets. . . ." Tom paused and looked down. He folded his napkin in half and then unfolded it again. "I was hoping to get to know some of them," he said, looking up.

Jennifer's look was not discouraging, but neither was it inviting. He took a breath.

Tom was the junior high pastor at their church, and Jennifer volunteered with the high school group. The two groups met on the same night, so Tom and Jennifer often saw each other. They also had gotten to know one another during the staff meetings and weekend leadership retreats held each year for the junior and senior high workers. They had never really had a lot of time to get to know each other on a personal level, but more and more Tom found himself noticing her comings and goings. After praying about his growing attraction toward her, he finally decided it was time to see where all of this might lead.

Jennifer looked across the room and then back at Tom. Her face was kind, but also apologetic. "I don't in any way want to be presumptuous, but I just want to be up front with you. I got out of a pretty rough relationship six months ago. I'm not sure I'm interested in any kind of relationship right now. I just don't want you wasting your time and energy. It wouldn't be fair."

Tom smiled and leaned back in his chair. He put his hands up as if to signal her to slow down. "I totally understand. I should have explained what I meant. I'm not interested in a relationship either, if what you meant by 'relationship' was what most people mean. That whole idea seems kind of goofy to me when I really stop to think about it. It's just that I don't know you that well and we don't have many opportunities to get to know each other, so I thought it might be nice to spend some time getting to know you better. And I need to be up front with you as well. I find you to be. . . ."

He paused, searching for the right word. Finally he came up with "interesting." *Interesting? Shoot. That sounded stupid.*

He went on. "I wouldn't have asked you out tonight if I didn't think that there might be the possibility of something more to our relationship than what there currently is—at least on my end."

Jennifer furrowed her brow. "I'm not sure I understand what you're saying. On one hand you're telling me you aren't looking for a relationship, and on the other you say that you find me interesting and would like to get to know me better. That seems kind of like a mixed message."

Tom smiled. "Yeah, I guess so. To be *really* frank, I'm not looking for a girlfriend; I'm looking for a wife. And," he quickly added, "I don't mean to say that that's for sure you."

He shrugged his shoulder. "Who knows? But that's why I want to get to know you. Look, it's like this. . . . Doing the whole boyfriend/girlfriend thing seems kind of pointless. I mean, where does that really get you anyway? It's just two people agreeing to like each other until they don't feel like liking each other anymore. There's no real commitment, and people end up giving their hearts away, and then the whole thing falls apart. I'd rather just stay friends with a person right up until engagement, since that's the only real commitment two people can make toward one another anyway. That way, if things don't pan out, no one gets as hurt. And if the relationship *does* lead to marriage, you haven't lost anything. So I don't plan on asking you—or anyone for that matter—for any kind of commitment. And since there's no promise I can make to a girl apart from the promise of marriage, I won't pretend to make one. I just want to get to know you better."

Jennifer was quiet for a moment and then finally said, "I can't decide if that's less pressure or more. It sounds like you're not asking me to enter into any kind of relationship at all, which to be honest sounds nice right now. But at the same time you're wanting to get to know me to see if you want me for a wife. What would happen if you decided you *did* want to marry a girl? Would you do the boyfriend/girlfriend thing then?"

"No. If I came to the conclusion that I wanted to marry a girl, then I would ask her to marry me, not ask her to be my girlfriend. Like I said before, I don't have much use for the whole dating relationship thing. I'd just move straight from friendship to engagement ... that's if *she* wanted to as well, of course," he added with a smile.

Jennifer didn't say anything, so Tom continued. "Really there's no pressure at all. I just want to become better friends. If at some point you know for sure that there could never be anything more than a friendship, just tell me, and that's all there'll ever be. And I'll do the same for you. In the meantime, feel free to date whom you want, do what you want, whatever. I don't want anymore right to dictate what you do with your life than I had yesterday. Let's just be friends and see what happens."

Finally Jennifer spoke. "I think I like the sound of this. And especially since coming out of my last relationship, the whole thing is beginning to make a lot of sense. But I'm not sure I totally get it yet. And since we're going to just keep being friends, the first thing I'd like from you is to keep explaining how this 'friendship to engagement' thing works. . . . It may come in handy some day."

Friendship: The "Non-Approach" Approach

So how does one go about finding a spouse if not by the typical means of dating?[1] What I propose here is neither complex nor particularly innovative. But its simplicity, I believe, is its greatest strength. In fact, I propose that we have no approach at all. It is the "Non-Approach" approach to finding a spouse.

Rather than moving from friendship to dating to engagement to marriage, I recommend that a man and woman move straight from friendship to engagement. With the Non-Approach, then, two people do not create a new category of relationship but rather develop a

> *So how does one go about finding a spouse if not by the typical means of dating?*

friendship prior to engagement. Its lack of novelty is perhaps what makes it novel. The main goal of the Non-Approach is to preserve the guidelines of sexual and romantic purity found in the Neighbor Relationship.

Note, however, that the advice given here applies only to those who are looking for a spouse. In other words, this is not my advice to parents on how to instruct their sixteen-year-old daughters in relating to young men. The guidelines of the Neighbor Relationship clearly define how a young man or woman should treat the opposite sex. What you will find here is a suggested method by which two people might intentionally move from one category of relationship to another without breaking the guidelines of either.

A Snapshot

The Non-Approach might look something like this: a young man and young woman are attending the same college. They have mutual friends and frequently spend time hanging out together in a group. After getting to know each other fairly well through this kind of interaction, it becomes increasingly clear that their mutual attraction and appreciation could potentially extend beyond the Neighbor Relationship. Rather than establishing a dating relationship, both the young man and woman agree to remain "just friends" and keep their relationship within the confines of the Neighbor Relationship. As they grow to know each other better, their mutual desire to move beyond the Neighbor Relationship will be either confirmed or denied. If it is confirmed, the two would move straight from the Neighbor Relationship to engagement, and then † Marriage Relationship as life opportunity permits.

Or perhaps, as in our opening vignette, the young man and woman do not really know each other well. The man appreciates what he sees in the woman and asks her out on a date. She says yes, and they enjoy an evening getting to know each other better. After some time, it becomes apparent that they are mutually attracted to one another, but they are not necessarily sure that moving into the Marriage Relationship would be wise. Like the couple in our previous example, they would agree not to create a new category of relationship but rather to maintain the purity guidelines of the Neighbor Relationship until they are sure they both desire marriage.

DISTINCTIVES OF THE NON-APPROACH

With this approach, I am adopting a minimalist strategy. In other words, my advice is limited to those elements of spouse finding that I believe are both logically and biblically essential to maintaining the purity of the Neighbor Relationship. Rather than focusing on the *goal* of spouse finding (what things to look for in a spouse), I will focus on the *process* (*how* to look for a spouse).

Though I believe Scripture allows for a lot of flexibility, four elements are crucial to any male/female relationship exploring the possibility of marriage: maintaining the guidelines of sexual and romantic purity in the Neighbor Relationship, communicating clearly, viewing dating as an activity rather than a category of relationship, and considering a relationship's exclusivity as voluntary.

MAINTAINING THE BOUNDARIES OF THE NEIGHBOR RELATIONSHIP

By declining to establish a new category of relationship, two people can more readily live within the guidelines of the Neighbor Relationship. The guidelines clearly detailed in 1 Timothy 5:1-2, as well as Song of Songs 2:1-7, are intentionally kept at the fore of the relationship and recognized as binding upon all "pre-engagement" male/female relationships. Both parties have an understood agreement that they will not cross these boundaries and that the requirements of purity for their relationship are no different than that of any other relationship.

In my mind, this truth alone almost necessitates the methodology described here in the Non-Approach. So much of our current dating (and even some courting) practices do not take seriously the scriptural mandate for sexual and romantic purity. The following distinctives flow out of a commitment to this foundational principle.

CLEAR COMMUNICATION

A crucial element of the Non-Approach, given its uniqueness, is clear and forthright communication between both parties. Likely one of the parties will not understand the concept of the Non-Approach, so it will be important to communicate one's purpose and intent in the relationship from the outset (as done in our opening vignette). For example, a woman who is operating under the traditional mind-set of dating would likely become confused by the actions of a man who had not communicated his commitment to the Non-Approach.

> *So much of our current dating practices do not take seriously the scriptural mandate for sexual and romantic purity.*

In keeping with the image of Christ's pursuit of the church, it would seem the man's responsibility to declare his interest in the woman as a potential marriage partner. If they have been friends for some time, he may already know for sure that he desires to marry her. If so, he should ask her. If he simply desires to know her better, this is all he should communicate. If she knows for sure that she has no interest in ever moving beyond the Neighbor Relationship, she can let him know immediately.

DATING AS AN ACTIVITY, RATHER THAN A CATEGORY OF RELATIONSHIP

We already discussed the distinction between dating as an activity rather than a category of relationship, so we need not belabor it here. Suffice it to say, however, that two people looking at each other as potential marriage partners do not, on the basis of their mutual attraction, have any grounds for establishing a category of relationship distinct from the Neighbor Relationship. Thus couples following the Non-Approach would view dating as an activity rather than a category of relationship. In other words, dating is something that two people *do,* rather than something they *are.* This distinction between dating as an activity rather than a category helps to maintain the truth that all unmarried men and women must relate under the guidelines established in the Neighbor Relationship.

The Non-Approach and Voluntary Exclusivity

Since no new category of relationship has been established, the exclusivity of the relationship can be only voluntary (self-imposed) rather than seemingly mandated by the relationship itself. True exclusivity is not possible apart from marriage or engagement. To think otherwise is a recipe for heartache.

This does not mean that a man and a woman cannot *voluntarily* choose to limit their interaction with the opposite sex. Not only is this permissible, I would recommend it. For example, if a young man is particularly interested in a specific woman, he will likely not want to spend time and energy developing signifcant relationships with other women. This would also be necessary for the sake of the women around him, lest he give them a mistaken impression about his interest in them.

A woman, likewise, may choose to turn down dates from other men when she knows that her interests lie elsewhere. But again, it is important to remember that there can be no real promise of exclusivity apart from marriage or engagement. So in the Non-Approach, each person is free to choose to be exclusive throughout the dura-

> *True exclusivity is not possible apart from marriage or engagement. To think otherwise is a recipe for heartache.*

tion of the relationship. The relationship itself cannot demand it. It may even be the case that a man will limit his dating activities to a particular woman, but she may not choose to be exclusive in return (or vice versa). More about the idea of voluntary exclusivity will be addressed in "Objections."

This lack of forced exclusivity goes a long way toward shattering the façade of "commitment" in pre-engagement relationships. As I have argued extensively in chapter 6, there can be no real commitment apart from a marriage proposal. Thus it seems wise to me that a man and woman would avoid using terms like "promise" and "commitment." Refusing to use such words in a pre-engagement relationship helps to maintain a proper perspective on the true nature of the relationship. Until a marriage proposal is offered and accepted, there can be no real commitment between an unmarried man and woman.

ADVANTAGES OF THE "NON-APPROACH" APPROACH

I believe the Non-Approach has many advantages, the first being its capacity to clarify the bounds of the Neighbor Relationship. This helps to protect individuals from the hurt that can come from premature romantic and sexual expression. It also allows two people to get to know each other without the distractions of a physical and romantic relationship, which in many ways can mask the true qualities of the dating relationship. Further, the Non-Approach is entirely consistent with Scripture. And finally, and most importantly, it helps to preserve the image of God that he intends our sexuality to portray. We will look at each of these advantages in turn.

THE NEIGHBOR RELATIONSHIP PRESERVED

The major advantage of the Non-Approach is that it in no way blurs the boundaries of the Neighbor Relationship. Because no new category of relationship is created or assumed, the familial aspect of the Neighbor Relationship is more clearly recognized and thus preserved. Even apart from biblical revelation, most Christians (and even some non-Christians) have a sense that the expression of romantic and sexual affection is out of bounds within the Neighbor Relationship. Understanding that two people are called to remain within the Neighbor Relationship until marriage is fundamental to a life of romantic and sexual purity. Remaining "just friends" until engagement keeps this boundary clearly before the man and the woman.

FREE FROM DISTRACTIONS

I would argue that there is nothing a person can discover in a dating relationship or courtship that cannot equally be discovered through a friendship. Life dreams, priorities, values, backgrounds, and character qualities can all be gleaned through a friendship. One does not need to establish a separate category of relationship to discern these things. In fact, I would argue that these important character qualities and life goals can be even more readily discerned within the context of a friendship.

Many dating relationships are based almost solely upon the romantic/physical attraction that exists between the couple. But strip this away, and they will discover that they have almost nothing in common and really nothing to talk about. If a couple cannot develop a friendship apart from a dating relationship, then marriage would be an ill-advised next step. But a friendship that is free from the dis-

> *If a couple cannot develop a friendship apart from a dating relationship, then marriage would be an ill-advised next step.*

tractions of a physical/romantic relationship has the opportunity to stand or fall on its own merit rather than merely being propped up by ebbing passion and desires.

FREE FROM HEARTACHE

Though no relationship can be totally free of heartache, the Non-Approach helps make heartache less likely. A friend of mine was introduced to a woman through a mutual friend, and the two of them initially hit it off. Committed to the basic principles of the Non-Approach, he expressed to me the unusual feeling he had as the relationship progressed. Used to jumping in with both feet, he found it both relaxing and comfortable getting to know a woman without the distractions of romance and a physical relationship. And after dating casually for a number of months, it became apparent to both of them that neither desired to move beyond the Neighbor Relationship.

They have instead remained friends, seeing each other on occasion without the regret that would have come from an aborted intimate, romantic relationship. He later confided to me that had the two of them become romantically and physically involved (as he had done in his prior relationships), it would have taken much longer to discern that there was no future in the relationship and it would have ended painfully for one or both of them.

This is not to say that feelings of disappointment can be eliminated entirely. Heartache may indeed arise for one party if the friendship never results in marriage. Disappointment and sorrow are legitimate feelings that should accompany the loss of any good thing. But all things being equal, the pain of loss within the Non-Approach is considerably less than the pain that comes from traditional dating relationships, for the Non-Approach has brought about an intentional attempt to maintain both physical and romantic purity.

CONSISTENT WITH SCRIPTURE

Not insignificantly, the Non-Approach fits well with the Bible's silence regarding finding a spouse. If God had wanted us to develop an official system by which we moved from one category of relationship to another, it seems likely that he would have informed us of it. Perhaps we should interpret his silence as an indication that he did not desire us to develop such a system.

> *Maintaining a friendship with a prospective spouse until engagement fits readily with the biblical expectations.*

Since the Bible does not prescribe a middle stage between the Neighbor Relationship and the Marriage Relationship, I would propose that we should be slow in doing so as well. Maintaining a friendship with a prospective spouse until engagement in no way impedes the future marriage and fits readily with the biblical expectations that God places upon men and women in the Neighbor Relationship.

PROTECTING GOD'S IMAGE

Most significantly, the Non-Approach helps to preserve the image of God that human sexuality is meant to express. When our children understand that no categories of relationships have been switched, the temptation to become romantically dependent and sexually involved is lessened. No shadow relationship of dating exists in which they can fall under the false assumption that it is safe and proper to begin giving themselves away. And this, of course, finds its ultimate necessity in the truth of Christ's single-minded devotion and affection for the church. Christ waited faithfully for his Bride, and thus we should teach our children to wait for theirs in a similar fashion. Christ fell in love once; we fall in love once. And the time for falling in love is engagement, not before.

The image of God that resides within our sexuality is of great value, and our desire to protect it is greatly serviced by refusing to create categories of relationships that appear to be distinct from the Neighbor Relationship and thus seemingly free from its commands of sexual purity.

Objections to the Non-Approach

In communicating this approach, I have encountered a variety of objections. Though by no means exhaustive, the following objections typify the general concerns that parents and young people have with the Non-Approach.

Objection 1: The Non-Approach is too insecure and vulnerable, since it lacks commitment

A young woman expressed her concern with the Non-Approach by saying, "Looking for a spouse requires you to open up and become vulnerable. I'm not going to bare my soul with some guy who is dating other women."

I would agree whole-heartedly with her concern. A woman would indeed be unwise to become vulnerable with a guy who was not sure what he wanted. Any man who is serious about a particular woman will limit his interaction with other women. But the woman he is interested in must remember that regardless of whether or not he is her boyfriend, any exclusivity is only self-imposed. To think otherwise is a breach of sound judgment. It does her little good to desire the security that comes from an apparently exclusive relationship when, in fact, such security does not really exist.

We must teach our children to enter into relationships with their eyes open, fully aware that man-made titles such as "boyfriend" and "girlfriend" in no way provide any real measure of security. The fact that two people openly acknowledge their attraction toward one another does not guarantee that such attraction will be permanent.

It is true that the Non-Approach offers no security, but its main advantage is that unlike dating, it doesn't *pretend* to have any. In my estimation, this makes it a much safer method. By not requiring exclusivity, the risks of finding a spouse are fully exposed. In a dating or courting relationship, the man or woman is able to walk away at any time. Doing so would in no way break any commitment. The man has not promised to marry the woman, and she has no right to expect that he will.

For a woman to feel that a dating or courting relationship offers a context in which it is now safe to become vulnerable is a feeling based on falsehood. Nothing is inherently more secure in a dating or courting relationship than in the Non-Approach. The more our children are aware of this, the more accurately they can make informed decisions about whom they will choose to become vulnerable with—and the more carefully they will guard their hearts.

Man-made titles such as "boyfriend" and "girlfriend" in no way provide any real measure of security.

I would argue that the self-imposed exclusivity of the Non-Approach is grounds for greater security than that of a traditional dating relationship. In the Non-Approach, a man chooses to limit his interaction with the opposite sex because he wants to. When a woman sees this exclusivity, she knows that it is sincere, freely chosen, and from the heart. In contrast, how is it more secure for a woman to believe the reason her boyfriend dates her exclusively is because the relationship requires it of him? When the exclusivity is recognized as voluntary, the woman is fully aware of a man's attraction toward her, as well as his unreadiness to make a permanent commitment. From this perspective, she now has the ability to make wise choices about how vulnerable she will choose to be with him.

Objection 2: The Non-Approach is unable to give enough information regarding the appropriateness of a future marriage

The idea that a dating relationship must be established in order to really know a person is, I believe, false.

"How are our children supposed to know if they want to get engaged to a particular person," one might argue, "if they do not develop a dating relationship first?" But does actively expressing their mutual attraction really help a man and woman discover whether or not they will be a good husband or wife?

Expressing one's sexual/romantic passion does not provide any useful information in determining the viability of a spouse; rather it can cloud one's ability to think wisely about the issue. Everything a person needs to know about another can be learned in a friendship. One does not need to give or receive sexual expression to know whether or not they want to do so. The idea that a dating relationship must be established in order to really know a person is, I believe, false.

OBJECTION 3: IT'S NOT REASONABLE TO THINK THAT OUR CHILDREN CAN TREAT A PERSON THEY ARE CONSIDERING FOR MARRIAGE AS "JUST A FRIEND"

Young people I have spoken with about the Non-Approach often initially find it difficult to think of a person they are considering marrying as "just a friend." And indeed, they are pursuing an agenda with that person that they do not pursue with other men and women. As a single friend of mine stated, "When I ask a girl out on a date, the fact of the matter is that I'm looking for something different in her than I do from my other friends that are women."

I would not at all contest my friend's observation. There really is a difference between the interaction a young man will have with a woman he is pursuing as a wife and the women he has no interest in. But this does not mean that such a relationship needs to step outside the guidelines of the Neighbor Relationship.

Clearly there are many sub relationships within the broad category of the Neighbor Relationship. Many of these relationships have very different agendas, purposes, and levels of emotional attachment. Business relationships, good friends, best friends, mere acquaintances, future spouses, even pastoral relationships all necessitate different types of interaction, intimacy, and emotional involvement, yet they all fall within the large category of the Neighbor Relationship.

The Neighbor Relationship does not insist that all relationships within it are the same, only that the guidelines of romantic and sexual purity are the same for each relationship. For example, though the interaction between a pastor and congregant and prospective husband and wife will entail different kinds of interaction, both relationships are called to keep their interaction within the guidelines of purity established by the Neighbor Relationship.

So without ignoring these distinctions, the Non-Approach asks only that all interaction between a prospective husband and wife be carried out according to the biblical guidelines of purity. The aim of the Non-Approach is not to pretend that such distinctions within the Neighbor Relationship (and hopes for marriage) do not exist, but rather to help both parties keep a clear perspective on what such a relationship does and does not entail. It *does* entail two people looking for a spouse. It does *not* entail two people who have already found one.

OBJECTION 4: THE NON-APPROACH ISN'T PRACTICAL IN TODAY'S SOCIETY

Since when do we determine truth based on practicality? Though the least spoken, this is perhaps the foundational objection leveled by many detractors of the Non-Approach. Often when speaking to parents or students, I encounter no resistance as to the content of what I am saying, yet I still encounter resistance regarding my conclusions. It is as though they agree with me, and even agree that the Bible seems to teach what I am suggesting, but the thought of actually trying to live out this ideal within our contemporary society seems so impossible as to be beyond reach.

> *Since when do we determine truth based on practicality?*

Jesus encountered this same situation when he taught on divorce. When his disciples were told that divorce was permissible only for marital unfaithfulness, they were astounded and exclaimed, "If the relationship of the man with his wife is like this, it is better not to marry" (Matthew 19:10, NASB). In Jesus' day, divorce laws were so lax that a man could divorce his wife for almost any reason. Jesus' teaching was so restrictive given the social context of his day that his command seemed almost to negate the whole idea of marriage. But the disciples' dismay arose from their lack of faith in the possibility of keeping Christ's commands.

Some may not agree that the Bible teaches what I am suggesting. If you find yourself among such, then you have the freedom of conscience to follow a different path. But those of us who have become convinced otherwise are bound by what we believe the Bible to teach. We cannot simply declare Scripture to be unpractical and then set it aside for something more expedient.

CONCLUSION

If the picture of the Non-Approach approach does not sound like it entails much romance or securi-
ty, keep in mind that experiencing romance and security is not its objective. All the romance, passion, intimacy, and security that our children long for is waiting for them

> *Dating relationships are really only shadow relationships that promise nothing concrete.*

in marriage. Dating relationships, though they may appear to provide these things, are really only shadow relationships that promise nothing concrete. Since no promise can be made apart from engagement, it would be wise for us as parents to encourage our children to establish relationships based on this reality.

This is the main reason that I propose maintaining a friendship as opposed to establishing a dating or courting relationship. It protects sexuality and allows the fruit to ripen on the vine so it can be enjoyed to its fullest capacity within the context of marriage. It is not slowly nibbled away in relationship after relationship, rendering unclear the single-minded nature of Christ's relationship with the church.

Regardless of what method you encourage your children to use as they pursue a spouse, keep before them the fundamental guidelines of the Neighbor Relationship. Any system that appears to remove two people from the confines of this relationship is misguided and creates potential for great harm to both your child and the image of God.

Discussion Questions

How would you explain the Non-Approach approach to a friend? What is its main goal?

What are the four crucial elements in any male/female relationship in which the couple is exploring the possibility of marriage?

What are the advantages to following the Non-Approach?

How would you answer someone who argues that the Non-Approach offers a couple no security?

Chapter 8

FOUNDATIONS FOR APPLICATION

SOME THOUGHTS ON THE HEART OF RULE MAKING

"If a law had been given which was able to impart life, then righteousness would indeed have been based on law" (NASB).

—*The Apostle Paul*

Bearing in mind that a significant element of sexual purity is found in refraining from arousing or awakening love before its proper time, we parents must give careful thought to the activities that we will allow our children to be involved in. These last few chapters address these issues based on our foundational principle that the sexual relationship between a man and a woman is meant to serve as a type of Christ's relationship to the church.

Let me say up front that following this advice will not be the secret to our children's holiness. God is the secret to our children's holiness, specifically, his grace poured out through Christ. Our children's passion for God will take time to grow. And because of this, it will be necessary for us to protect them from consequences of their immaturity until they are able to stand on their own. But we must not rely upon rules and worldly restraints to restrain the desires of the flesh. This is the heart of legalism and empty religion. We must trust wholly in the sufficiency of Christ's risen life, striving with all our heart, modeling with all our life, and praying with all our faith that our children might first learn to love God above all else. It is love, not rules, that give birth to obedience. When we teach our children to love God, their obedience will follow.

Before we discuss the rules we may want to set for our children, let's take a look at what Scripture has to say about the place of rules as they pertain to holiness. As those called to "image" God, we do well to use rules and laws in a manner similar to God himself. For as we come to understand the way in which God uses laws and rules, we will have a pattern for our own use of laws and rules as we strive to birth purity in the lives of our children.

> *When we teach our children to love God, their obedience will follow.*

Using Rules like God Would

Many in the church today share a common thought that somehow holiness is achieved by avoiding tempting circumstances. Nowhere is this thought seen more readily than in our effort to arrive at sexual purity. Most books and sermons I have read or heard on the subject seem to mistakenly suggest that the secret to sexual purity is to avoid sexual temptation: get rid of the TV; don't go to the pool; don't thumb through the Sunday paper.

This concept fosters a rules-centered Christianity whereby the main goal of our faith is to avoid anything that might provoke us toward wickedness. But this is such a shortsighted understanding of biblical righteousness and holiness. Though we should take wise and necessary measures regarding our environment, we must not rely upon them as the final solution to sexual purity. If the only way we can arrive at sexual purity is by manipulating our environment, then we have completely missed God's greatest gift in overcoming sexual temptation: the power of the Holy Spirit. Righteousness is not achieved by avoiding sinful environments but by embracing Christ. It is the indwelling presence of the Holy Spirit that births holiness in our hearts.

> *Righteousness is not achieved by avoiding sinful environments but by embracing Christ.*

So as we contemplate the rules we will set regarding our children's purity, it is important that we understand their proper place in achieving sexual purity.

JUSTIFIED BY THE SPIRIT, NOT BY LAW

The apostle Paul dealt extensively with the subject of legalism and rules in the book of Galatians, and this New Testament book is a treatise on the power that Christians now have in Christ. In this letter, particularly chapters 3 and 4, Paul instructs his readers about the nature and purpose of the Old Testament Law. This Law (found in the first five books of the Old Testament) provided the moral and religious foundation upon which Jewish believers based their lives. The Law was extensive, dealing with personal and corporate holiness, governmental structure, and ceremonial cleansing, among other things.

But the coming of Christ changed the way in which the people of God related to the Law. No longer, Paul says, are we "kept in custody under the law" (Galatians 3:23, NASB). As we look at Galatians, we discover that with the indwelling presence of the Holy Spirit, the Law's usefulness in God's overall plan had come to a end. Understanding how and why this came about is paramount to a life of Spirit-empowered obedience and will give us an important pattern for our own use of rules. To begin to understand the relationship between Law and holiness, we must understand why God gave the Law in the first place. Paul explains the purpose of the Law in 3:19, where he states that it was "added because of transgressions." In what way did our transgressions necessitate the addition of the Law?

I believe the Law served as a temporary, external hedge that helped to maintain the purity of God's people until the coming of Christ and the regeneration that followed.[1] Paul describes the Law as a babysitter or tutor (3:24), whose job was to protect God's people from the sinful influences of the surrounding nations. In other words, God's people required the Law because they were spiritually immature and unable to maintain holiness in the face of temptation. The message of the Old Testament Law was not, "Go into the world and convert it" but rather, "Come out from the world and be separate" (and sometimes, in essence, "Go into the world and slay it, lest it corrupt you"). The Law separated Jewish believers from the world, since as yet God had not provided the means by which they could mean-ingfully interact with it without becoming tainted by its poison. The Law's very presence indicated that those in need of it were still in infancy, regardless of how perfectly it was kept.

The Galatians, having at one time understood the sufficiency of Christ alone for salvation, were mistakenly relying upon the external influence of the Law to produce an inward experience of holiness. They thought that by avoiding certain actions and embracing various ceremonial practices, they could achieve true righteousness. "Are you so foolish?" Paul asks in Galatians 3:3. "After beginning with the Spirit, are you now trying to attain your goal by human effort?" Both they and we need to often be reminded that the way to holiness is not through adhering to a strict legal code that attempts to separate us from evil influences ("Don't smoke, chew, or go with girls that do!").

Holiness comes through the new life found in the justification of Christ. In Galatians Paul teaches that the indwelling presence of the Holy Spirit renders the Law unnecessary. With the spiritual rebirth of the New Covenant, we are no longer spiritual children and thus no longer in need of a babysitter. In the Old Testament,

> *The way to holiness is not through adhering to a strict legal code that attempts to separate us from evil influences.*

the people of God were controlled externally by the Law, but now in the New Testament, we are controlled internally by the Spirit. This is the source of true power and the ability to live a godly life. More than rules and laws, your children will need this power if they are to live purely and righteously in this fallen world.

An Earthly Example

You as a parent may have a list of rules that you expect your young children to follow: clean your room; take out the trash; gather your laundry; brush your teeth; don't cross the street alone; save part of your allowance. You may likely include a system of rewards and punishments as they follow (or don't follow) the rules that you have clearly spelled out.

Without carefully explaining these rules and making sure that your children followed them, your children would make themselves miserable. They do not have the inward maturity or strength of character to govern themselves. But if your child at the age of twenty-one cannot decide for himself when it is safe to cross the street or needs to be told to brush his teeth, something has gone wrong!

The rules you set are not to be permanently relied upon but rather to lead your children to the place where they no longer need them. Adults do not brush their teeth because they are compelled by an external source but because of their internal desire. The same principle holds true, I believe, for how Christians relate to the Old Testament Law. As New Testament saints, we no longer rely upon an extensive list of dos and don'ts, telling us how we should behave toward God and each other. We are under the Law of the Spirit.

Jesus, Paul, and James all explicitly affirm the command to love as the sum total of the all-revealed Law (Luke 10:25–28; Romans 13:9; James 2:8). Because of the Holy Spirit, we do not need an elaborate list of commands to know how love should be carried out. Rather it is much more intuitive, flowing from who God has made us (and *is* making us) in regeneration and sanctification. It is the foundational aspect of the fruit of the Spirit, the ability that comes to all who are born of God (1 John 3:14; 4:7).

> *The rules you set are not to be permanently relied upon but rather to lead your children to the place where they no longer need them.*

We are fundamentally different people than the Old Testament believers. New Testament believers' lives should be marked by a higher level of holiness and love than the Old Testament believers, for we possess the salvation that they could only see from afar (1 Peter 1:10–12), the salvation that the Law itself was leading us toward (Romans 3:21).

This is not to say, however, that even we as New Testament saints have entered into the fullness of our inheritance. Paul tells us that the Holy Spirit is a "deposit," the firstfruits of the perfection that is to come at the Resurrection. Thus we exist in a sort of spiritual dawning. The sun has risen in our lives but has not yet come to its full zenith. In this regard we still need "rules" and "laws" from God, and the New Testament is not devoid of these. But it is clear from even a simple reading of Scripture that God's call to obedience is much more clearly detailed and formalized under the Old Covenant than that the New.

No other subject tends to breed legalism more than sexual purity. So often I see people try to achieve sexual purity mainly by avoiding tempting circumstances. Traveling with a companion of the same sex when on business, asking the hotel staff to block the cable to your room, and refusing to go into stores that prominently display inappropriate material are all wise measures. Why place ourselves in the way of temptation?

But if such actions are the *only* way we are able to avoid sexual impurity, we have not yet embraced all that God offers us. The hope of the gospel is that God will not only forgive us our sins but actually deliver us from them as well. Our goal for our children should be for them to become the kind of people who will choose purity even when presented with the opportunity to sin. But if the only way we train them to avoid sin is by avoiding its opportunity, this goal will never become a reality.

As Paul readily acknowledges, abstinence from evil can never secure holiness. Holiness is more than just the absence of evil; it is the presence of a love for God, which comes only by the Spirit.

Like the Old Testament Law, our rules cannot "impart life." We can develop an extensive list of prohibitions and commands, but in the end, if our children have not grown into the maturity afforded by the Spirit, our rules have availed nothing. Rules for our children are necessary, just as the Law was necessary for children of God during the Old Testament age. But

> *Our goal for our children should be for them to become the kind of people who will choose purity even when presented with the opportunity to sin.*

relying on an external list of rules can be only temporary. Our real goal as parents is to introduce our children to the transforming power of God's grace. And it is through their deepening union with Christ that this grace becomes a reality in the lives of our children.

OTHER THOUGHTS ON RULE MAKING

With this understanding of the function of rules, we have a proper foundation upon which to use rules as a temporary hedge to protect our children. In the next chapter we will deal with specific situations such as dances, movie choices, and music, but let's take a moment to consider some general thoughts regarding rule making that we as parents might consider as we attempt to lead our children into the life-giving power of the Spirit.

SHORTENING THE ROAD

So much of our secular culture is specifically designed to do the very opposite of what Scripture mandates. It is becoming increasingly difficult for a young person to live a life of sexual purity that bears well the image of God. A hundred years ago, a young person

> *So much of our secular culture is specifically designed to do the very opposite of what Scripture mandates.*

might not have begun thinking seriously about the opposite sex until the early teens. And it was not at all uncommon for a young couple to marry at the age of seventeen or eighteen years old. So from the time a young man or woman began to desire the opposite sex until the time when he or she could actually consummate that desire would often be less than five years.

In today's culture, however, sexuality is being fanned into flame in children even as young as five or six years old. Children's movies are just one example of this. The Walt Disney movie *The Hunchback of Notre Dame* portrays, in part, the story of a man who burns with fiery lust for a beautiful, seductive gypsy woman. The man's lust and obsession for the woman drives him to the point where he attempts to murder the woman in order to be free from his lust for her. And this was billed as a *children's* movie!

Not only is sexuality being thrust upon our children at a younger and younger age, the typical age for marriage is being pushed back to the mid and late twenties. So where there used to be a five-year season of waiting, there is now a twenty- to twenty-five-year season of waiting. The road to purity is getting longer and harder. We should expect that this trend will only continue, and we must be prepared to protect our children from it as much as possible. We must help them not to "arouse or awaken love" until they are at an older age, and we must work to prepare them for the maturity of marriage at a younger age. Our culture has lengthened the road. The intent of our rules should be to shorten it.

Regardless of the difficulties that this world presents, we cannot eradicate the sin from our culture, and we cannot hide from it. We and our children are called to live in it without being tainted by it. Teaching them how to do this is the goal of parenting. We will not be able to hold our child's hand throughout her entire life, and if the first time we let it go is when she leaves for college, we will have ill prepared her for the road ahead.

My father told me that one of his main parenting goals was to teach me how to make good decisions. The ability to make good decisions comes only from practice, which will necessarily include times when our children make poor ones. While our children are still under our authority and protection, we need to begin to slowly loosen the bonds, giving them the freedom to stand or fall by their own choices. In this way they will learn to make decisions for themselves when the consequences are not nearly so severe and we are still there to pick up the pieces.

But unless we have given them the proper tools with which to handle this freedom, we cannot hope that they will use it wisely. Ultimately our goal is not to get our children to *behave* as God desires them to but rather to *desire* as God desires them to. If they view the world from a God-centered perspective, they will invariably make right decisions. This reminds us of our need to birth within our children first and foremost a love for God and his image.

Start Early to Create Healthy Expectations

I remember as a sixteen-year-old the expectations I carried into my first dating experience. I had been friends with a girl for a few years, and when I found out that she liked me beyond the state of our current relationship, I was immediately interested in moving the relationship along. She lived out of state, so our relationship consisted mostly of phone calls and letters.

After one of my few visits, she informed me that her father was concerned about our physical relationship. I was astonished and indignant. We had been "dating" for five or so months and had merely snuggled together on the couch and shared one brief kiss goodnight. (And I was pretty sure her father didn't even know about the kiss.) Compared to the physical relationships of my dating friends at church, this was saintly. I remember thinking, "Good grief. What's the point of being boyfriend and girlfriend if you can't snuggle and kiss a little? If we were any less physical, we would be just friends!"

Looking back, I am grateful to her father for his wisdom and caution. And I see clearly now that my expectations were seriously askew as I entered into relationships with members of the opposite sex (both romantic and not). I had grown to *expect* that I would have some measure of physical/sexual relationship with my "girlfriend." I cannot help but wonder how my relationships with girls would have been different if I had started from an early age to hold the conviction that I would not pursue a physical or romantic relationship with a girl until I was ready for marriage.

It will be easier for a child to accept the principles of God's Word if he or she is instructed in them from a young age and did not spend years fantasizing about a physical/romantic relationship prior to marriage. Imagine if you told your child that you would get him a car for his sixteenth birthday, but then you changed your mind at the last minute. This would be more difficult for him to accept than if you had told him all along you would get him one for his eighteenth birthday. It is a matter of expectations. The longer our children expect to have a physical/romantic relationship prior to marriage, the harder it will be for them to accept the fact they should not. If you are a parent of a preadolescent, you have a tremendous opportunity now to begin shaping the expectations of your child. Don't wait until your child has already put the boat in the water before you tell him or her it is too soon to set sail. Start young.

> You have a tremendous opportunity now to begin shaping the expectations of your child.

Basing Rule on Faith, Not Fear

The motivation behind the rules we set is just as significant as the rules themselves. If we are panicked by the sin in the world, our children will be panicked by the sin in the world. Ultimately this kind of panic is driven by fear, fear that what is in the world is greater than he who is in us. When we panic about movies, TV, and music, we are communicating to our children that we do not believe the Holy Spirit is strong enough to withstand these temptations.

Consider a mother who is watching television with her young son. During a commercial break, a provocative lingerie commercial comes on. The mother jumps up and quickly switches the channel. Turning to her son and fixing him with a piercing look, she says, "You don't need to watch that! Just erase that from your mind!" as though she were angry with him. What she has just communicated is that it is not possible for a man to see a scantily clad woman without lusting (which isn't true and insults the power of God's transforming grace) and that sexuality is evil and should be avoided at all costs.

Now imagine the same situation, but this time the mother calmly switches the channel and mildly says, "Oops. We don't need to be seeing that." And then perhaps with a wink toward her son she says, "Victoria should keep that secret to herself and her husband." What she has just communicated through her calmness is that the need to switch channels isn't primarily about her son's inability to refrain from lust (though there may yet be some reality to that) but rather because the model's sexuality should not be shared so openly. Further, she has communicated that sexuality is a good thing, which is the reason it should not be shared so openly. And her calmness communicates that she does not believe sin to be overpowering, which in turn gives her son confidence that he can overcome temptation.

> *If we subtly communicate to our children that pervasive sexuality cannot be witnessed without lusting, we set them up for almost certain failure.*

If we subtly communicate to our children that pervasive sexuality cannot be witnessed without lusting, we set them up for almost certain failure. There will come times in their lives when they will not be able to keep from witnessing a man or woman who insists upon expressing their sexuality inappropriately. In those moments, they must be able to withstand the temptation. Joseph is a great example of this. We can presume that he, as a wise man, stayed away as much as possible from Potifer's wife. But in the end, he could not avoid her, and it was his self-control that delivered him from evil, not his ability to avoid a tempting circumstance.

We must teach our children that though they should avoid tempting circumstances, they do not need to be afraid of them, for the power of God within them is greater than the power that is in the world.

So as we consider the rules and restrictions that we should wisely place upon our children, it is important that we do not act out of fear. If the sin and depravity of the world terrifies us, perhaps we ourselves do not believe strongly enough in the power of God. Our children will sense in our fear a lack of confidence in God's strength to deliver from temptation, and they will behave accordingly. God is strong to save. We must believe it.

Parenting, Fulfillment, and the Image of God

During a seminar with parents, a father asked me what he might do to help teach his sons self-control regarding their sexuality. The question is a good one and gets to the heart of the issues we are addressing. Self-control is born out of satisfaction. When we are not satisfied, we insist upon seeking pleasure in illegitimate ways. Ultimately only the knowledge and experience of God can fully satisfy. If our children are to live lives of self-control and sexual purity, they must be satisfied enough with God that they are content to live without the legitimate pleasure of sexual gratification for a season (or perhaps even a lifetime).

> *We as parents must understand our God-given responsibility to our children as the primary image-bearers of God.*

This is where our role as image-bearers fits in. Children first receive their knowledge and experience of God from us as parents. The thought lingers in my mind that an entire book could be written about parenting and its connection to the image of God! But without diverting too far from our main subject, it is of supreme importance that we as parents understand our God-given responsibility to our children as the primary image-bearers of God. Following are just a few thoughts on this important subject.

Heavenly Father, Earthly Father

In the Old Testament a man could beat a slave or attack a neighbor without incurring significant repercussions under the Law. For a child to merely *speak* ill of his parents, however, resulted in the death penalty (Exodus 21:17). Paul affirms the need to honor one's parents, as well, in Romans 1:28–32, where he lists disobeying one's parents alongside murder and the "invention of evil." He finishes the discussion by stating that those who do these kinds of things (such as disobeying their parents) deserve death.

Why such harsh words of condemnation? I believe the answer is found in the idea that parents, above and beyond anyone else, serve as the primary image-bearers of God to their children. When a child rejects the headship of the parent, he or she is rejecting in the deepest way the headship of God. God demands that children honor their parents because the parent represents God to the child in a way that is not possible in any other relationship. How are we to understand the fatherhood of a human parent if not as the image of God's eternal Fatherhood? And conversely, how is a child to understand God's Fatherhood if not through the image she sees in her own father?

This should be a sobering reality for us as parents. We have not just been *given* responsibility for our children; we really *are* responsible for our children. To a great extent, they will become what we make them, forming their opinions about God primarily from what they see in us. When we fail to live out the image of God, our children will likely be dissatisfied and will be drawn toward sin and temptation.

The child with an abusive father will have great difficulty conceiving of a heavenly Father who loves with gentleness. The child who sees his parents unable to love one another unconditionally will struggle to imagine a God who loves unconditionally. And when our children fail to see in us an adequate picture of God, they will fail to be satisfied, for satisfaction is found only in the knowledge and experience of God. They will search for it elsewhere, likely in the next most obvious place: the opposite sex.

> *Parents communicate what God is like by how they interact with each other, their children, and the world around them.*

Ultimately no other human relationship more closely resembles our relationship with God than that which typifies it, the relationship that exists between a man and a woman. The temptation to make an idol of this relationship is avoided only by a real and vibrant knowledge of God.

And there can be no hiding our failures. Our insecurities leak through. Even if a specific sin of ours is kept secret from our children, the insecurity that led to the sin cannot be hidden. It will be intuitively revealed to our children, and our inability to find satisfaction in our relationship with Christ will lead them down their own road of dissatisfaction. The child whose father successfully hides a pornography addiction will still struggle with lust (or some other expression of dissatisfaction) even if he has no knowledge of his father's struggle. For though the sin itself is hidden, the insecurity that gave birth to the sin cannot be. And since the father has not found a meaningful experience of God, he cannot pass it on to his child. He can pass on only what he possesses: his insecurity.

Our children come into the world as needy, empty vessels, and it is our job to image forth for them the all-satisfying vision of God.

BE YOUR CHILD'S SPOUSE

It is said that sons tend to marry women like their mothers and daughters tend to marry men like their fathers. While this may not always be accurate regarding *personality* traits, a correlation usually can be seen in the *character* traits of the grown child's spouse and those of the parent. Daughters who have experienced abusive relationships with their fathers tend to end up with husbands who are abusive. And sons whose mothers nag and are high-strung tend to end up with wives who are the same.

Why is this? I believe the answer relates back to the image of God that parents possess in relation to their children. Parents communicate what God is like by how they interact with each other, their children, and the world around them. As I stated earlier, what children perceive about God through their parents will have a significant impact on their own sense of security. The areas in which parents fail to convey the image of God leaves in their children's hearts an emptiness that those children often try to compensate for through a relationship with the opposite sex. But as they seek to fill up this emptiness, they look for the image of God that they already know through their parents. Consequently, they end up pursuing the same image they saw in their parents—as limited as that image is. I do not think that this accounts for all the reasons why children tend to marry people like their parents, but the fact that this happens should be grounds for a moment of sobriety on our part.

Since your child will likely marry someone who shares your character traits, let this be a motivation to become the kind of person that you would desire your child to marry. Fathers, if you want your daughter to marry a strong, godly, compassionate man, then this is what *you* must be. And mothers, if you want your son to marry a confident, trusting, and loving woman, then this is what *you* must be. Pray earnestly that God would continue to make you into the kind of person that you desire for your child. This starts now, while they are young. By the time they are in their teens, you will likely have already formed their expectations of what they will look for in a spouse.

We must keep in mind that *who* we are as parents is far more important than what we do or the rules we set. We can set the proper boundaries for our children, but if we do not fulfill our role as an image-bearer of God, we will have only given the skeleton of holiness without the heart.

> *When we explain the "why" of God's commands, we invariably explain God himself.*

There is great hope for parents who drink deeply from the fountain of God's grace, even if they haven't read the latest how-to books. Above all, we must be right as men and women of God, bearing his image well and then praying like crazy that God would open the eyes of our children to experience through us the sufficiency of Christ.

We will not be perfect, but by God's grace we can image forth the beauty and goodness of God more often than not. The past is done, and the future lies before us. If we have failed in the past, we must lay it aside and start fresh. We cannot undo the past, but we can still shape the future. What we meant for evil, God intended for good, so even in our failures we must not despair, for God is able to wrap them in the cloak of his sovereignty and work them for the good of those who love him and have been called according to his purpose.

CONCLUSION

My father was once asked about the key to parenting success. He answered simply by saying, "Prayer and the sovereignty of God." This is not to say that we parents don't play a vital role in the purity of our children, but it is quite true that apart from the grace of God in our children's lives, there is no hope that they will ever honor him. Our task as parents is not to merely instruct our children in rules but rather to reveal to them a picture of the God in whose image they live.

All of God's commands are given to us that we might know what he is like and worship accordingly. When we teach our children about the connection between marriage and Christ's relationship with the church, for example, we have not only given them rules to live by, we have revealed to them God's love for his people, God's power to save, and the hope of new life. When we explain the "why" of God's commands, we invariably explain God himself.

All of God's rules are meant to direct us back to his own nature, which teaches us about who he is and ultimately increases our love for him. Give your children merely rules and ideals, and they will not even desire holiness. Give them a knowledge of how those rules fit with the character of God, and they will crave to follow the rules in order that they might find the God of those rules.

Discussion Questions

What was the purpose of the Old Testament Law? Why are believers today *not* under the Law?

How can parents begin to teach their children to make good decisions?

Who is a child actually rejecting if he or she rejects the headship of the parent? Why is that so?

Considering that a grown child often marries an individual with character traits similar to one of their parents, what character traits in yourself do you need to adjust?

Chapter 9

DANCE, DRESS, MOVIES, MUSIC, AND MORE

THINKING BIBLICALLY ABOUT PRACTICAL ISSUES

"Whether you eat or drink or whatever you do, do it all for the glory of God."

—*The Apostle Paul*

Ahh . . . the many and varied choices that parents must face regarding the sexual purity of their children. In this chapter we will discuss a few of the major issues that most parents must face at one time or another. Helping our children stay pure through all the muck that this world has to offer is no easy task. Can we protect our children from social dangers and the world's sexual licentiousness without moving our families to a commune in Montana? I think we can, but we must not take lightly the obstacles that would prevent us from raising pure children in an impure world. This calls for much wisdom, prayer, and a desperate dependence on God.

As we begin to think about the structure that we will give to our children's social and entertainment lives, I would like us to focus on two important ideas. First, let us keep in the fore of our minds the mandate that our children are not to "arouse or awaken love until it so desires" and how this command relates to the image of God. Just as Christ has reserved his affection for his heavenly spouse, we too are to each reserve our affection for our earthly spouse. Christ fell in love once; we fall in love once. He unites himself spiritually with none other than the church; we unite ourselves sexually with none other than our spouse. All of the rules we set for our children should strive to produce in them these realities.

Second, teaching our children discernment should be our primary parenting goal. It is not our chief duty to merely protect our children from harmful environments. We must also teach them discernment so they will be able to navigate their own ways through this fallen world. We must remember that our children are called by God to engage and change the culture. If our main agenda in life is to hide our children from the sin of the world, we will do a poor job in preparing them to be the ambassadors of Christ that they are called to be. We cannot hide them in the basement until they are eighteen and then expect them to be prepared to effectively serve Christ when they leave home. Protection and exposure. A careful balance between the two must be maintained.

It will be impossible to teach our children discernment without letting them gradually interact with the fallenness around them. But as they begin to grapple with the sin in the world, we as parents have a responsibility to be by their side. Just as it is not our job to hide our children from the culture, it is not our job to throw them to the culture to face it on their own. We need to be there with them, teaching them to think properly about what they are observing and experiencing. This will require parents and children to "do life together" and necessitates open communication. In the end, we desire them to "be as shrewd [or wise] as snakes and as innocent as doves" (Matthew 20:16).

> *Protection and exposure. A careful balance between the two must be maintained.*

LOOKING AT THE ISSUES

The intent of this chapter is not to dictate what you should do but rather to raise concern regarding some of the more troublesome issues that we all encounter, particularly in light of what we have discussed regarding sexuality and the image of God. Some of the subjects we will address relate to clear biblical principles, while others are perhaps a bit more subjective. In the end, it is your responsibility to provide direction for your children regarding these and other issues. And it is your responsibility to help your children understand the intent of any rules that you might impose. Don't just tell them things like, "We don't watch those

> *Give your children the "why" of the rule, and it will be easier for them to submit to the rule itself.*

kinds of movies" without explaining how that decision relates to a desire to protect the image of God. Give them the "why" of the rule, and it will be easier for them to submit to the rule itself.

DANCES

We're not in Kansas anymore! So much has changed regarding what is socially permissible in the sexual arena. We need only to look at regular network programming to see that the level of graphic sexual content has increased dramatically over the last twenty-five years. This "freedom of expression" unfortunately is not limited to TV. Clothing, dance moves, and the overall focus of typical school dances seldom affirm the message that you will be trying to teach your children about sexual chastity and self-control.

While I cannot know the environment of every dance your children might attend, the overall intent of a dance itself is to provide a romantic atmosphere in which young couples can spend an evening together. In light of God's command not to "arouse or awaken love" until the time is right, we must give careful thought to our children's involvement in such an activity. Granted, many students attend dances in groups or without dates and are looking only to have a good time with friends. This does seem to make the whole thing a little more benign in my mind, but I cannot escape the feeling that often the nature of a dance is counter to what I want my kids to know and believe regarding sexual and romantic purity.

CHECK IT OUT FIRSTHAND

There is no better way to assess the nature of a dance than by observing one yourself. Undoubtedly the local school administration will be open to this (particularly if you volunteer as a chaperone). This is the course my father took when I asked to attend a "sock-hop" after school in junior high. After having attended the dance as a chaperone (with me in attendance), he told me that he felt there were no real benefits to gain from my being there and saw many potential dangers. I was not old enough to fully understand the dangers he saw, but I reluctantly bowed to his wisdom. I consequently did not attend dances during my high school years. Though initially I found it embarrassing to explain to my friends that my parents did not allow me to attend school dances, as I grew older I adopted their perspective for myself, and I was grateful for their wisdom in this area.

GIVE THEM FREEDOM

If you decide against allowing your children to attend dances, you may at some point want to give them the opportunity to take ownership of that conviction. As I neared the end of my high school years, my parents gave me the freedom to decide for myself whether or not to attend prom. Thinking through the expense and focus of the night, I concluded that I wasn't really interested in attending. By that time, I had taken ownership of the decision and freely told my friends that I just didn't want to go. Though I did not at that time fully realize the significance of the image of God or the need to refrain from arousing or awakening love, I had come to the point where I saw little advantage in involving myself in the activity.

> *If our children choose the right path only because we have forced them to, they will leave that path as soon as our authority is absent.*

It is wise to withhold this freedom until our children are mature enough to handle it. Placing this freedom before a junior higher is likely not fair to your child. And knowing that we will be giving them more freedom as they grow older should remind us of our need to not merely communicate proper behavior but to instill proper desires. If our children choose the right path only because we have forced them to, they will leave that path as soon as our authority is absent. But if our children begin to choose the right path because we have taught them to desire it for their own sake, our influence will carry throughout their entire lives.

Regardless of the decision you make regarding dances, devote to it much prayer and talk openly and honestly with your children. Whether you choose to allow them to attend dances or not, the subject provides a great opportunity to talk about purity and the image of God. Be sure that your children understand what it is about a dance that is inconsistent with God's ideal. If in your context the dangers of a dance outweigh the benefits, don't be afraid to follow your conscience. I fear that too often parents simply go with the flow and are not willing to put themselves in the unpopular position that comes from making a counter-culture decision. We must not be weak in the leadership that we give to our children's pursuit of purity. They are counting on us. Before you say yes or no, consider the following questions:

- Have I observed firsthand the environment that my child will be facing at this dance?
- What benefits will my child gain from attending the dance?
- What potential dangers may my child encounter at the dance regarding their sexual purity?
- Does allowing my child to attend the dance send a mixed message about sexual purity?
- Have I talked with my child about the ways in which certain aspects of a dance can be inconsistent with God's ideal for sexual and romantic purity?
- Will this event make it difficult for my child to "not arouse or awaken love" before its proper time?

DRESS, NUDIST COLONIES, NUDE BEACHES, AND CLOTHING CHOICES

If I had to guess, I would bet you are opposed to your children joining a nudist colony or frequenting nude beaches. As a matter of fact, so am I. But why? Is it because the temptation to lust will be overpowering in such an environment? Nudists assure us that public nudity is not about sexual desire. It's about freedom and an appreciation of nature. To some extent I believe them. (The thought of watching a bunch of naked people play tennis in nothing but socks and gym shoes arouses my sense of humor much more than my sexual desire!)

Though viewing outright nakedness on a grand scale may initially invoke a measure of sexual desire, the more people expose themselves to such an environment (pun intended), the less effect it will have on them. What may initially prove exciting will gradually lose that excitement as it becomes commonplace. And this, I believe, is precisely the problem with public nudity—not that our children would be tempted to sexual desire but that public nudity would actually hinder this capacity.

Sexual desire is good, and God created the sexual parts of our bodies to arouse sexual desire. But when we render them as common, we rob them of their power to function in the way that God designed. The problem with public nudity is not primarily that it leads to lust but rather that something sacred is being treated as something common. To take the sexual parts of our bodies and treat them as casually as we do our arms and fingers is an affront to what God intended them to portray and hinders their capacity to function in the way that God designed.

> *To take the sexual parts of our bodies and treat them as casually as we do our arms and fingers is an affront to what God intended them to portray.*

Keep in mind the image of God that our physical sexuality communicates. When a man and a woman come together bodily, they are imaging forth the spiritual union of Christ and the church. And when a man looks with desire upon the nakedness of his wife, he images forth accurately the desire that Christ has for his Bride (though Christ's desire for us is by no means sexual). Sexual desire, in its proper context, is good and beautiful. But like alcoholics, who can drink more and more without getting drunk, nudists become increasingly calloused to the sexuality of those around them. Seeing a naked man or woman becomes mundane. This is a bad thing. The ability to control sexual desire should come from the power of the Spirit, not from having become so calloused to sexual stimuli that we no longer find it stimulating.

CLOTHING CHOICES AND MODESTY

Now I didn't really think that many of you were wrestling with the viability of public nudity, but I raised the issue as a segue into something more common: our children's clothing choices. The purpose of clothing is to protect our sexuality, to keep the sacred from being treated as common.[1] Just as fine china is reserved for sacred occasions, so too the erotic aspects of sexuality should be reserved as a means of communicating the deep spiritual relationship between Christ and the church.

When we protect our sexuality, it is able to function in the way God intended. But this particular subject can be a seedbed of potential conflict for parents and their children, since how they dress will likely be hugely significant to them. (We will look at this issue mainly from the perspective of parents and daughters, since controversy with sons in this area usually has to do more with looking sloppy or a similar issue.) Compounding the potential for conflict will be the likely naiveté of a girl's awareness of her own sexuality. In her mind, she will not choose her clothing because it makes her look sexual

> *We must not sacrifice the image of God for the sake of style.*

but because it makes her look attractive and in style. The problem arises when the styles of the day are less than modest. Here are a few things we might want to consider as we help our daughters think through the appropriateness of their wardrobes.

CONSIDER THE GOAL

Ultimately clothing is to protect the sacredness of our sexuality, not only for our sake, but for the sake of God and his image. But I fear that we are often like the frog in the kettle, unable to discern how hot the water has become until it is too late. What we Christians deem permissible by today's standard would have been condemned by the world fifty years ago. Let us think soberly about this. Just because we dress more modestly than Hollywood does not mean that we are dressing modestly. Keep in mind that a woman's need to dress modestly is not mandated simply to keep men from stumbling into lust but rather to protect the image of God that she possesses through her sexuality. Modesty is for her sake as much as the men around her. She is not to share or offer her sexuality to anyone but her husband, just as Christ does not offer himself to anyone but his Bride.

But this is not at all the intent in many of today's fashions. In fact, just the opposite is true. Much of women's clothing purposely draws attention to a woman's sexuality. But the body was made for the Lord, to be given to only one. And though our daughters may not always agree, it is possible for them to dress in a manner that preserves their modesty without making them look out of style. We must not sacrifice the image of God for the sake of style.

Maintain Balance

We could, of course, take this line of thinking to an extreme. We would end up with a society not dissimilar to an Islamic society, covering women from head to toe, not letting them out of the house. So I readily acknowledge that there is a need for balance in all things, lest we get carried to extremes. But I would suggest that we as a society (even a Christian society) are a long way from becoming overbalanced toward excessive modesty.

In the end, I believe it should be our goal as much as possible to make clothing a nonissue. We do not want our children to dress in such a way that they attract undue attention to their sexuality, but neither should they dress in such a way that they are unable to function in the world that God has called them to minister to. Clothing should not enhance our sexuality, but neither should clothing give the impression that we are ashamed of it. As you prayerfully think through this issue, consider these concerns.

- Does my child's outfit draw overt attention to her sexuality?
- Does my child's outfit help protect the image of God within her?
- Does allowing my child to wear this particular outfit send a mixed message about sexual purity?
- Will this outfit make it difficult for my child or those around her not to "arouse or awaken love" before its proper time?
- Have I talked with my child about why modesty is important?
- Am I helping my child develop an attitude of discernment in the clothing she wears?

Music, Movies, and TV

The entertainment industry wields a powerful influence, and I fear that it affects our families more often than we realize. In some ways I worry that we have become so accustomed to the world's standards that we no longer view the entertainment industry's message with any kind of discernment. It should come as no surprise that the secular entertainment industry is counter to much of what God stands for regarding purity. (Bear in mind that the issue of purity involves more than just refraining from premarital intercourse; it also involves romantic purity.)

Having said this, however, I am not suggesting that we bury our kids' heads in the sand. What I am suggesting is that we parents need to enter into this world with our kids, keeping a critical eye toward truth and God's ideal. It would be tremendously unwise of us to turn our kids loose to the entertainment industry without supervision. But until we ourselves have the ability to think critically about these issues, we will not be able to teach our children to make wise choices. So my goal is to highlight a few of my concerns with the various entertainment mediums, specifically music, movies and TV.

Music

Our culture has replaced God's image with that of mankind's, and this is often readily seen in the secular music industry. Words that should apply only to God are often sung about the relationship between a man and a woman. Not long ago I heard a man expressing in a love song his deep need for a woman, assuring her that if he had her love, his life would have purpose and meaning. He would not fear death, for he would know that her presence would follow him. He went on to confess that he was nothing apart from her and that her love made him whole.

It should strike us immediately that a Christian cannot truthfully sing these words to anyone other than God. The relationship between a man and a woman is meant to be the image of God's relationship with his people, but the world has allowed the image to eclipse the real thing.

Not every love song is like this, but if we listen closely to the lyrics of secular songs, we will find that many do not speak of love and romance in ways that are consistent with God's image of Christ and the church. The singers are worshiping each other rather than God. Even simple love songs that are not overtly sexual in nature are often contrary to the image that God would have us display through our romantic lives. This, of course, goes without saying for music that is overtly immoral in nature. Songs that celebrate premarital sex and licentious behavior obviously have no place in the Christian's life. They are not just subtly inconsistent with the image of God; they are blatantly opposed to his image.

If we are not careful, the message of these songs will be not only implanted in our minds but also subtly imbedded in our hearts. If day after day we—or our children—unknowingly fill our minds with a message that is inconsistent with God's ideal, it is likely we will be negatively influenced by

> *What we model will almost surely be the end result of our children's own discernment.*

it. The messages of many secular songs are counter to a life of physical and romantic purity. Are we teaching our children to carefully discern the message of the songs they listen to? Even more importantly, have we taught them the truth of God's ideal in such a way that they have embraced it for themselves, giving them an inward shield against the lies of this world?

MOVIES AND TELEVISION

Before we talk about what we should allow our children to watch, let's take a moment as parents to evaluate what we allow *ourselves* to watch. What we model will almost surely be the end result of our children's own discernment.

The viewing side of the entertainment industry is so full of unrestrained sexuality that it is often hard to find a movie or TV show that doesn't portray something deeply counter to the image of God. It embarrasses me now when I think about the movies that I would watch as a young man with barely a twinge of conscience. My friends and I would watch movies with a PG-13 or an R rating that would invariably include a sex scene, and we would merely say, "Don't know why they had to put *that* in there." It was as though as long as we mildly lamented the fact that the scene was in the movie, it was then permissible to watch it.

It's Not Just Acting

In my mind, sex and nudity on the screen is more destructive than gratuitous violence. The violence we see on the screen is acting. No one is really being maimed or killed. But nudity on the screen is a completely different matter. When we see actors naked or scantily clad, they are not just pretending. They *really are* naked or scantily clad. Likewise, when we view a graphic sex scene, the actors are not just pretending to kiss and fondle one another; they *are* kissing and fondling one another.

If someone were to sit in a bedroom and watch a couple make love, even with their permission, you would call that person a voyeur and think that his or her actions were wrong. Does it make it any less wrong if the couple is unknown and is on a movie or television screen?

One might try to argue (as I did) that he or she isn't watching the movie for the sex scene. This may be true, but we seem to always end up watching the sex scene anyway. Do we really think that we will get up and walk out of the theater if a sex scene starts? If we were that committed to purity, we probably would have checked out the content of the movie beforehand.[2] In some movies, the actors' revealing clothing is so pervasive throughout the movie that it would be impossible to look away at the appropriate times without missing half the movie. Again, we should look away not simply to avoid lusting but out of respect for the image of God that resides within the actors. Even though they are not respecting their sexuality, our respect for Christ should cause us to do so nonetheless.

Just as we would respectfully look away from a woman whose blouse was accidentally torn, so too we should look away from a woman who chooses to expose herself on screen. Ultimately what we value in both cases is the image of God that resides within a person's sexuality.

Don't Miss the Message

Graphic sexual context aside, many movies and television shows portray a message regarding sexuality that is inconsistent with God's ideal. It is perhaps a bit too simplistic to restrict your children's viewing based on whether or not a certain show or movie includes a sex scene. Like we observed earlier regarding music, a message is conveyed with each movie and television program. As yet, evening sitcoms do not contain complete nudity. Yet many shows continually portray sexuality in a way that is inconsistent with God's image. We must be very careful that we do not allow our desire to be entertained to overcome our desire to grow in our sensitivity toward God's ideal.

> *Our children's convictions will mirror our own.*

Are we willing to throw off everything that hinders? Until we are willing to do so, it will do us little good to do it for our children. We cannot wait until our children have been put to bed and then watch television programs or movies that we do not allow them to watch.[3] The hypocrisy will be so blatant that our children will not be able to miss it. Having convictions ourselves about what is appropriate to set before our eyes is the quickest way to create convictions in our children. Their convictions will mirror our own.

Talk to Your Children

In spite of all the garbage, cutting our children off completely from all secular music, TV programs, and movies is probably not the best course of action. Again, I would stress the need to teach our children discernment. To some extent this will involve engaging the world in some form or fashion. But communication is of utmost importance. Don't simply invoke a ban on secular media without helping your children understand the ways in which it can often be counter to the image of God.

Many times my father would listen to a song with me and then talk about the message it portrayed. Sometimes the message affirmed God's ideals and sometimes it did not. If he felt that a song was particularly harmful or misguided, he would ask me not to listen to it anymore. Our open dialog and his supervision allowed him the opportunity to teach me to evaluate the worth and value of such things.

And finally, we must not be afraid to be the parent. Some movies, songs, and television programs are simply not worth the sacrifice of purity that they entail. There were many movies that my parents did not allow me to watch, and I believe I am better for it. Their stance communicated to me that their value system was built on a different premise than that of the world. Communication and explanation is the key. So as you begin to talk to your children about what they should be watching or listening to, here are some questions that may help provide clarity.

- Am I willing to make sacrifices for the sake of my children's purity, even if it means giving up my favorite TV shows, movies, or songs?
- What benefits will my child and I gain from watching these shows or movies or listening to these songs?
- What potential dangers may my child and I encounter regarding our sexual purity in listening to these songs or watching these shows or movies?
- Does watching this show or listening to this song, or allowing my child to do so, send to my children a mixed message about sexual purity?
- Will these songs, movies, or shows hinder my child's efforts to "not arouse or awaken love" before its proper time?
- Are these songs, movies, or shows creating wrong expectations for my children regarding relationships with the opposite sex?
- Do I take opportunities to discuss with my children the message of the different entertainment mediums?

MASTURBATION

Though not necessarily a topic that is easily talked about even in adult (especially in adult?) company, it is important that we discuss the subject of masturbation with our children. It is an activity they will almost surely explore at some point in their lives, and for many young people, both men and women, it will become a form of sexual addiction. Though the Bible does not address the subject directly, we can say a number of things about it.

Reasons to Relax

I believe that the Bible's silence regarding masturbation should be an indication of exactly how significant of a subject we should make it. Though explicit sins often accompany masturbation (use of pornography, lustful desires, illicit sexual fantasies), it is difficult to state with certainty that masturbation in and of itself is a sin.

Certainly the Bible does not blush at awkward topics. The Old Testament mentions bestiality, homosexuality, and incest—to name a few. Had God felt that masturbation was an extremely significant issue, it is likely he would have mentioned it directly. In light of this, I do not believe that we need to make the subject of masturbation in and of itself a major issue for our children regarding sexual purity. Almost all children will experiment with it, and though I do believe there are Biblical reasons to discourage the practice, we need not make our children feel any more shame than they will likely feel on their own. It will give them comfort to know that for most well-adjusted people, the desire to masturbate lessens with the years. The desire is perhaps, more than anything, merely a mark of emotional and spiritual immaturity, losing its grip as a child grows in Christ.

Reasons for Caution

However, there are a number of reasons we as parents should be concerned about the issue. Often the desire to masturbate is born out of lustful thoughts and desires. When masturbation is done within this context, it is clearly displeasing to God. But the real sin here is the sin of lust that gives birth to, and is increased, through self-gratification. As mentioned earlier, our children must learn to harness and control their sexual appetite, not arouse and express it outside a marriage relationship.

Second, masturbation is sinful when it becomes a form of sexual addiction, a substitute for the presence of God. Ultimately all sins are symptomatic of a deeper issue. An addiction to masturbation is no different. The young person (or adult) who is addicted to masturbation is looking to meet deep relational needs that can be met only in God. Should you find your child is addicted to masturbation, more than just actions are the issue. It will do your child little good for you to simply tell him or her to stop. Rather, we must help our children find a meaningful relationship with Christ that drives away the desire to masturbate.

We cannot exist in a vacuum. We are finite creatures who long to be filled, and it is our nature to search restlessly for relief. When we are not filled with Christ himself, we will search to fill ourselves

Our children must learn to harness and control their sexual appetite, not arouse and express it outside a marriage relationship.

with other things. For young people, and still many adults, masturbation provides an immediate sense of relief from this sense of unfulfilled longing. But the relief it brings is only temporary. A prolonged addiction to masturbation can serve as an indicator to the observant parent that something is missing in the child's life.

But perhaps what our children needs is what we ourselves still lack. The father who has yet to find a significant, satisfying relationship with Christ and struggles with his own addiction should be little surprised to discover that his son is struggling as well. We must plunge deeper into the grace of Christ before we will be able to help our children.

And finally, masturbation does not fit well at all with the image of God that he intends our sexuality to portray. As we observed previously, God intended the physical oneness of the sexual relationship represent the spiritual oneness of Christ's union with the church. As a type then, masturbation falls short of this reality, for it is an act that is devoid of relationship. It is using sex as a means to self-gratification apart from the gratification of another. It is an inherently self-centered affair. Sexual activity in this fashion cannot serve as an earthly type of the heavenly reality.

To use our sexuality apart from the context in which God created it is to use it inappropriately. Masturbation can never be satisfying either sexually or spiritually, for it does not find its meaning in the higher reality of Christ and the church.

Conclusion

As I mentioned previously, rules will not secure our children's holiness and purity. We can eliminate all traces of inappropriate content from our children's lives and still have children who grow to be addicted to pornography.

In the end, holiness comes only from an experiential, firsthand encounter with the life-changing person of Christ. Rules and structure are important, but if they are all we give our children, they will be no better off than the Pharisees. Our children must learn to love God with all their heart, soul, mind, and strength.

> *Holiness comes only from an experiential, firsthand encounter with the life-changing person of Christ.*

The rules and restrictions that we place upon them are merely temporary stopgaps until their love for God grows. This love will take some time to develop, and their enthusiasm for their sexuality will likely precede their enthusiasm for God. Thus it is important that we as parents protect them from their desires until their love for God can take over. May God give us wisdom as we seek to set responsible boundaries for our children.

Discussion Questions

When is the proper time to begin giving children more freedom?

Consider one rule that you have placed on your child. How can you explain to your child the reason for that rule?

Reflect on the music you normally listen to, the television shows you watch, and the movies you view. You may even want to go further and think about what you read. Now consider that children often mirror their parents' convictions. What might you need to change in your viewing, listening, or even reading habits?

LIVING BY FAITH

TRUSTING THE HAPPINESS OF GOD

*"I am confident of this very thing, that He who be-
gan a good work in you will perfect it until the day of
Christ Jesus."*

—*The Apostle Paul* (NASB)

The subject of sexuality is submerged in passion and significance.
It matters a great deal to almost everyone. And the stakes are very
high, not only as they pertain to our own happiness, but also as
they pertain to the glory and image of God. The path of the world
is broad and many travel upon it. The path of the cross, however, is
narrow and few find it. Those who do are often misunderstood and
mocked. If you have become convinced of the connection between sexuality and the image of God and understand the need to
direct your children away from the world's patterns, I implore
you to stand firm in the truth of God's Word. It will not be without a
temporary cost, but the end for both you and your children will be
blessings in both this life and the life to come.

Stand firm in the truth of God's Word.

Undoubtedly, not everything I have written in this book is wholly of God's wisdom. I trust, however, that much of what I have said is close enough to God's ideal that he will use it to assist you and your family as you strive to live for him.

BOUNDS OF THE NEIGHBOR RELATIONSHIP

From an application standpoint, I would reiterate this important truth: the bounds of the Neighbor Relationship are binding until marriage. If you can convince your children of this, the majority of the remaining details will ultimately fall into place: dating as a category of relationship will be either abandoned or redefined, the physical and romantic boundaries will be objectively understood, and the timing and intent of romantic relationships will be clear from the outset.

However, if we allow our children to operate under the mistaken assumption that a dating or courting relationship is excluded from 1 Timothy 5:1-2 and its standard of absolute purity, we open them up to a world of subjectivity. Help your children live within the clearly defined categories of the God-ordained male/female relationships, and they will have the objective truth they need to live lives that honor God.

SEX, THE GOSPEL, AND THE IMAGE OF GOD: THE "WHY" OF GOD'S COMMANDS

If there is one message that I have desired most to convey, it is this: sexuality is about the image of God. Indeed, *all* of life is about the image God. This is the joy and hope of mankind. Everything we see, every thought we think, every action we take should point us back toward a knowledge of God. And thanks to God's Son, there will come a day when this entire world will conform itself to the pattern that God intended. We will live in a world that conveys in all things, at all times, the goodness of God's glory and nature.

Sexuality is just one facet of this image. In this present life it points us toward so many aspects of God: it proclaims the hope of the gospel, speaks of our union with Christ, and reveals the goal of our salvation. It is as valuable as that to which it points. Only time will tell what use our sexuality will have in the eternal Kingdom. But just as it has been ordained in this New Testament age to reflect the glory of Christ's relationship with the church, I believe it will evolve in the coming ages to point us toward those aspects of God that have yet to be revealed.

Make it your goal to live out your sexuality in a way that is consistent with the nature of God. And make it your goal as parents to help your children live out their sexuality in a similar fashion. In God alone is happiness, for he is the essence of happiness itself. Trust in this happiness, for it is only when our lives are conformed to the image of this happiness that we can know true joy.

The Hope and Despair of God's Ideal

And finally, the commands of God, particularly in the realm of the heart, should shatter our sense of self-sufficiency. The path to which God calls us is beyond the realm of human effort—it simply cannot be attained apart from divine assistance. Yet his commands should inspire in our hearts a sense of expectation and hope, for those commands reveal the heights to which God will take us as we look to him in faith.

> *The Lord does not command that which he does not enable.*

We cannot live out our sexuality in a way that is pleasing to God—let alone teach our children how to do so—apart from grace. And this grace is the very thing that God supplies us through Christ. Even as I finish this book, I am overwhelmed again by the standard to which God has called us in all areas of our lives and humbled by the many ways in which I seem to fall so short. But as Augustine has prayed, "Give what you command and command what you will." For the Christian, the Lord does not command that which he does not enable.

So if you find the road too long, then rest assured that you have found the right road. With mankind, this journey is impossible; but with God, all things are possible. He remembers our frame, that we are but dust. His mercy and grace are sufficient for our failures along the way, both for us and our children. Neither you nor your children will be able to perfectly live out his image. So we must strive for the ideal with all our hearts while affording ourselves the same grace that God has granted to us through Christ. Our children will not be able to perfectly guard their hearts, but

> *For the believer, the battle is already won.*

they can *consistently* guard their hearts. And God's purpose in our lives is to make us more obedient. So let us and our children keep our eyes on his face, rather than our own stumbling, and press on toward the goal of God's ideal. For the believer, the battle is already won; it merely remains to be fought.

Rethinking the Gospel

Understanding the importance of our spiritual union with Christ

I believe the connection between sex and the gospel is seldom made in today's Christian circles because we have long minimized the most significant element of our salvation—our spiritual union with Christ. Too often we speak of the gospel as merely the good news of God's forgiveness, as though forgiveness is all that sinners need to enter the kingdom of heaven.[1]

We will never view the sexual relationship as an image of the gospel until we understand that the gospel entails more than just the forgiveness of sins. Indeed the Bible clearly teaches that forgiveness alone is not sufficient for entering into eternal life. If we find that statement shocking, we must remember that the gospel is not merely the message of God's forgiveness but the good news of regeneration through our spiritual union with Christ. When we understand and keep this element of the gospel firmly in mind, we will be able to see how sex is a "type" of the gospel, providing an explanation for why God created it in the first place. In turn, this view will give us a solid foundation upon which to understand sexual purity.

The Necessity of Spiritual Regeneration

Christ makes it clear that a primary requirement for inheriting eternal life is that we actually be alive. "Unless one is born again," he said, "he cannot see [or enter] the kingdom of God" (John 3:3, NASB). Paul explains why this is so in Ephesians 2:1–3: when we were sinners, we were "dead in [our] transgressions and sins" and "we were by nature objects of wrath." No other word in the Bible better describes the fallen and bent condition of humanity than the word "death." Biblically speaking, to be spiritually dead is to be separated from God and thus separated from all of his goodness. And it is this corruption of our very nature that makes us culpable before God.

In other words, even apart from any evil work that we do, we are condemned before God because of our very being. We are by *nature* objects of wrath. Fundamentally, it is essential to understand that what keeps us out of Heaven is not only what *we've done* but even more significantly *what we are*.

Paul makes this point in the magnificent book of Romans, one of the clearest statements of the gospel in all of Scripture. In Romans 5:13-14 Paul shows that our fundamental source of culpability before God stems from our condition (spiritual death) even apart from any of our actions (breaking God's commands):

> Before the law was given, sin was in the world. But sin is not taken into account when there is no law. Nevertheless, death reigned from the time of Adam to the time of Moses, even over those who did not sin by breaking a command, as did Adam, who was a pattern of the one to come.

Note Paul's main point here: spiritual death has been the condition for all people apart from Christ, *even for those who did not break any of God's commands!* Paul explains that after Adam and prior to the Old Testament Law, "death reigned," even though no law had been given that could be broken (v. 14). So though the people who lived between Adam and Moses did not sin by breaking a command, they were still condemned before God due to corruptness of their spiritual death.

For example, imagine an angry man whose heart is filled with murderous hatred. This man lives alone on a deserted island. As such he never murders anybody. But his refraining from murder is not due to the fact that he is godly. Quite the contrary, he simply lacks opportunity to express what is in his heart. So though he is not a murderer by action, he is a murderer by nature. In the same way, those who lived prior to the Law were still accountable to God as sinners even though sin was "not taken into account when there [was] no law." They were condemned before God as lawbreakers, not because of their actions, but because of their dead, fallen nature. Had the Law been present, they would have broken it immediately.

Paul makes it clear in the remainder of this passage (vv. 15–19) that the condition of spiritual death is the primary reason that Adam's descendants are under God's condemnation. Paul uses the expression "condemnation" and "death" interchangeably throughout the passage. In 5:17 he writes, "For if, by the trespass of the one man, *death reigned through that one man,* how much more will those who receive God's abundant provision of grace and of the gift of righteousness reign in life through the one man, Jesus Christ." In the next verse Paul summarizes the statement by writing, "Consequently, just as the result of one trespass was condemnation [i.e., the spiritual death mentioned in verse 17] for all men, so also the result of one act of righteousness was justification that brings life for all men."

Ultimately then, it is our dead, sinful condition that separates us from God, not simply the fruit of such a condition. This is why a person must be born again if he or she is to enter into eternal life. But how is it that anyone is born again? Does God simply remain aloof and far removed, pronouncing us "alive" from his throne in Heaven? No, rather he comes to us through the living Christ, uniting us to his very own life through his Holy Spirit. We are born again because we have "become one" with One who is the essence of life itself. The words of both Paul and Peter make this truth plain.

THE NECESSITY OF SPIRITUAL UNION

The apostle Paul highlights our spiritual union with Christ as the primary hope of the gospel and the source of spiritual regeneration. In Ephesians 2:4 and 5 he writes, "Because of his great love for us, God, who is rich in mercy, *made us alive with Christ* even when we were dead in transgressions—it is by grace you have been saved."

Note here that the salvation Paul speaks of is spiritual regeneration through Christ. This is what he means when he writes, "By grace you have been saved." In other words, it is because we are "with" Christ that we participate in his life and thus are saved. Paul makes the same point in Colossians 1:27, where he tells us that "Christ in

[us]" is our hope of glory. It is through our spiritual union with Christ that we partake of his life. We are born again precisely because we have become one spiritually with the life of Christ through the joining of our spirits.

The apostle Peter also tells us plainly that it is through our spiritual union with Christ that we escape the corruption of this fallen world and inherit the promise of eternal life. Read his words in 2 Peter 1:4 (NASB):

> He has granted to us His precious and magnificent prom-
> ises, in order that by them you might become partakers
> of the divine nature, having escaped the corruption that
> is in the world by lust.

Through our union with the divine nature, we escape the corruption that is in the world—namely our condition of spiritual death (v. 4). When Scripture speaks of our spiritual oneness with Christ, it is referring to our union with the divine nature. Through Christ our finite, frail human nature has been wedded to the infinitely powerful divine nature. This is the essence of our salvation, and it is this union that is our hope. As noted earlier, the sacraments of both baptism and communion also demonstrate this profound spiritual reality and highlight the necessity of our spiritual union with Christ.

THE TWO ADAMS

We have been "born again" into a new nature, wed spiritually to the very Son of God. This then is our hope—not that God will simply make us perfect people like Adam before his fall, but that God will make (and is making) us perfect people who are permanently united with the divine nature through the indwelling of the Holy Spirit, according to the image of the infinite Son. When at the resurrection our salvation is complete (Philippians 1:6), we, like Christ, will have infinite power to do all that God calls us to.

Mercy, as good as it is, is meant for only this age. God is preparing us for the day of his kingdom, when we will no longer need mercy because of all that he has made us through his grace. And it is through our spiritual union with Christ that such a future becomes a reality. When we are saved, the very life of God through Christ via the Holy Spirit has taken up residence inside us. We have become irrevocably wed to the divine nature. Sex within marriage presents a powerful symbol, or image, of this unseen union.

IMPLICATIONS FOR APPLICATION

FURTHER THOUGHTS ON LIVING OUT THE IMAGE OF GOD

The ways in which we think about and act out our sexuality must always be influenced by a knowledge of its intended purpose. When we understand what sex is intended to illustrate, we are armed with the information we need to live lives pleasing to God. The knowledge that God has ordained sex as a means of portraying the image of our spiritual union with the divine nature has many implications for both us and our children. Not only does it provide the "why" and the "how" of sexual purity, it also explains why sexual sins are so destructive. It informs us about the holiness of sex, and it acts as a God-centered motivation for pursuing sexual satisfaction. This appendix will look briefly at these three further implications.

THE SEVERITY OF SEXUAL SIN AND THE BLESSINGS OF PURITY

The fact that sexual union serves as a type of the gospel reveals why sexual sins have so much potential for harm. That which has the potential for the greatest good also has the potential for the greatest pain. The severity of sexual sin is seen clearly in the fall of church leaders and clergy members. A pastor can struggle with pride, greed, or laziness but not necessarily find his job in jeopardy. But the pastor who sins sexually will almost always find the door.

Is this unfair? Is it wrong for us to make such a big deal about sexual sins and treat nonsexual sins as less significant? I used to think so, but as I have come to understand the importance of sex and sexuality, I have become convicted that this natural inclination is just and proper. When people sin sexually, they sin against the deepest part of themselves, ultimately undoing the image of God in the most destructive manner. Sexual sin is so destructive because it strikes at the very core of all that God intended us to be as image-bearers of this divine glory.

In the Old Testament Law, a hierarchy of sins existed. Some sins could be atoned for by sacrifice and guilt offerings. The value of the sacrifice was directly proportionate to the destructiveness of the sin. The greater the sin, the greater the sacrifice. But some sins could never be atoned for, sexual sin being among them. The penalty for such sins was death. In fact, sexual immorality is listed along with murder and apostasy as one of the few things that an Old Testament Jew could do that would invoke the death penalty.

In 1 Corinthians 6:18 Paul demonstrates that sexual sin is indeed set apart as more significant than other sins. In this context, Paul rebukes the Christians at Corinth who were visiting prostitutes. This was a common practice in the city at that time, and apparently some Christians did not see this as inconsistent with their faith. After commanding them to abstain from visiting the prostitutes, Paul explains the extreme necessity to flee from sexual sins: "Flee from sexual immorality. All other sins a man commits are outside his body, but he who sins sexually sins against his own body."

Here Paul clearly separates sexual sins from "all other sins." He states that the consequences of sexual sins are against our own bodies. In some mysterious way, sexual sins cut to the very heart of what we are as people in a way that no other sin can. This is why it is so important to help our children make wise choices concerning their sexuality. Sexual sins are so damaging because they strike at the heart of the gospel. When we damage our sexuality, we damage our ability to see salvation in a clear and meaningful way.

Perhaps this is what Paul meant when he said that sexual sin is against our own bodies. Children who have been protected sexually and raised to be sexually pure will have a much easier time understanding and embracing the beauty of their relationship with Christ. Because their sexuality and the image it portrays are pleasing and beautiful to them, they will find it easy to believe that the source of that image (Christ's relationship to the church) is pleasing and beautiful. But children who have been violated sexually or have been sexually promiscuous will likely have more obstacles to overcome as they seek to embrace all that they have in Christ.

Mercifully, in this New Testament age, God's grace can and does cover sexual sin, but the destruction that sexual sin can cause is not always easily undone. It is not my desire to heap guilt upon those who may have sinned sexually in the past. In Christ there is no guilt. But as parents, we must fully understand the severity and damage that sexual sin causes, specifically as it relates to a young person's ability to embrace the gospel. God can redeem any person, including his or her sexuality, but though the wounds are healed, the scars may remain until the resurrection.

THE HOLINESS OF SEX

The relationship between sex and the gospel also has implications regarding the holiness of sex. Though we as Christians often give lip service to the wholesomeness of sex, this is not always born out by our attitudes toward it. We often speak of our sexual desire with a hint of shame and subtly give the impression that an interest in sex for the sake of sex is unhealthy. I believe this comes from watching the world muddy the pure waters of sexuality for so long that we in the church have developed a tendency to view sexual desire as evil and base. The world has perverted sex, making an idol of it. It is a substitute for the God they reject. We as Christians see this and intuitively know that this idolatry is wrong. But rather than seeing past the abuse, we often find it easier to throw out the baby with the bath water. Better to just reject it wholesale, we think, rather than try to clean it up.

I see this perspective when I hear Christians talk about the dangers of "sex, alcohol, and drugs." The implication seems to be that sex is as destructive as alcohol and drugs. That we can lump something good and pure like sex with something that has no redeeming value, like drugs, is a subtle indication about how we really view sex. Though the majority of us do long for sexual gratification, many still struggle with the underlying feelings of guilt and misgiving that accompany this desire. Many struggle to embrace their sexual passions as a healthy and God centered part of who they are. But the message that sex is barely permissible does not come from God or the Bible.

The knowledge that God has ordained sex as an expression of the gospel must always be kept in the forefront of our minds. Though the world has perverted it and used it for its own ends, sex itself is still something that God delights in. He greatly desires our sexual satisfaction and longs for us to know the joy that comes from being united to one another, for through such joy comes the ability to see the heavenly joy of being united with Christ.

Our children must be taught that sex is a good thing. But they must also understand that it is good only when it is first about the glory of God. When sex paints the picture of our union with the divine nature, it has the tremendous ability to be as satisfying as God intended.

The Necessity of Sexual Satisfaction

And finally, the fact that sex acts as an illustration of the gospel has implications about our need to enjoy it. Not only are the husband and wife called to sexual faithfulness, they are called to sexual satisfaction, to rejoice and be exhilarated within their sexual relationship. It is not merely a suggestion from God, but a command. Notice below in Proverbs 5:18-19 (NASB) Solomon's use of such words as "rejoice," "satisfy," and "exhilarated." From the context of the preceding verses, we see that these words are in reference to sex in particular, not just the marriage relationship in general.

> Let your fountain be blessed, And rejoice in the wife of your youth. As a loving hind and a graceful doe, Let her breasts satisfy you at all times; Be exhilarated always with her love.

Remember, the primary reason we are to be sexually faithful in marriage is because our sexual relationship is a picture of our union with Christ. Christ is faithful to his Bride, thus we are to be faithful to ours. For this same reason, sexual satisfaction within the marriage relationship is not optional for the Christian. The entire book of Song of Songs is a testimony to the pleasure that should exist within the sexual relationship between husband and wife. It is the duty of a husband and wife to enjoy each other sexually. An unhappy sexual relationship paints a poor picture of Christ's oneness with the church. Would we portray the image of a Christ who does not enjoy being one with his bride?

That sex is a picture of Christ's oneness with the church must also influence the way in which we find sexual satisfaction within marriage. God does not desire sexual satisfaction alone but rather sexual satisfaction in a way that correctly portrays his image. The way in which a husband and wife enjoy each other sexually must not stand in contrast with how Christ enjoys the church.

This is important for us to talk to our children about as well. We must not send them off to the marriage bed with the impression that as long as they are both satisfied, it doesn't matter what they do in their sexual relationship. Many sexual activities seem to be in contrast with the image that God intends sex to communicate. Sexual sadism (or even feigning sexual sadism), for example, does not portray well the way in which Christ relates to his church.

The duty to have a fulfilled, Christ-centered sex life in marriage highlights two important truths. First, sex is not only about our pleasure. We cannot choose to abstain from sex if we are married in the same way that we can choose to abstain from chocolate or exercise. We are commanded to satisfy each other sexually, for our sexuality is part of the image of God. Second, God's insistence that married couples be sexually satisfied shows the purity and sacredness of sex. Sex is sacred because God created it to image forth the very heart of the gospel. It is as pure as the gospel.

Our bodies are not for ourselves alone. As Christians, we have a double duty to honor God with our bodies. We are bound to honor him first because we were created to bear his image. And further, we are bound to honor him because he has bought us with the blood of his Son. I cannot stress this point enough: sexual purity, as well as sexual satisfaction, is first about the image of God.

Our children need to know that God intended the physical oneness of sex to be a picture of the spiritual oneness that exists between Christ and the Christian. And our children need to know that we as husbands and wives are satisfied in our sexual relationships. They will be able to see it intuitively, even if we try to hide it or don't speak of it. And what they sense about our sexual relationships will begin to shape not only their own views about sex but also their views about God and salvation.

Appendix C

Courting as a Dating Alternative
The strengths and weaknesses

Dissatisfaction with current dating practices has become increasingly widespread, and I am by no means the first to question the wisdom of such approaches. In the vacuum that has followed, the idea of courting has seen a renewal, particularly with the advent of Joshua Harris's book *I Kissed Dating Goodbye* and his follow-up book, *Boy Meets Girl*.

The popularity of Harris's books and the widespread defection to courting in recent years is an indication of the dissatisfaction that many have with the status quo. I believe that this resurgence of courting has been movement in a positive direction for our Christian culture. But though I find courting to be a significant improvement over the typical dating relationship, I would like to offer a few cautions regarding this approach. Not every type of courtship will be open to the criticism that I express here. Rather this is a critique of courting in general, highlighting the practice's strengths and weaknesses.

Before we discuss positive and negative aspects of a courting relationship, it will be helpful to establish a working definition of the term for those who are perhaps not as familiar with the practice. A couple is said to be courting when a man seeks to develop a formal relationship with a woman for the purpose of marriage, having declared his intention at the outset.

For some the term "courting" will have very conservative connotations (close parental involvement, curfews, not being alone without a chaperone), and for others it will mean no more than the definition I have offered. In fact, this basic definition comes close to the "Non-Approach" approach I recommended in chapter 7. Regardless of the various trappings that may accompany different forms of courting, a common element in all courting is the intent of the activity: marriage. This is perhaps the main ingredient that sets courting apart from a typical dating relationship. It is essentially dating with the clear objective of marriage as its goal.

THE PROS OF COURTING: A MATTER OF TERMS

One main advantage that I see in courting (as opposed to a dating relationship) is an issue of meaning and terms. Courting is generally regarded as an activity, whereas dating has become increasingly associated with a *kind* of relationship. When we say that a couple is dating, most interpret this designation of the couple's relationship as something unique and separate from what we intuitively know as the Neighbor Relationship. But if we say a man is courting a woman, we understand it to mean that he is seeking her hand in marriage. Will she decide to remain in the Neighbor Relationship, or will she consent to move into the Marriage Relationship? This helps to maintain the biblical guidelines regarding physical and romantic purity. Since courting does not necessarily establish a new category of male/female relationships, the biblical ideals are not so readily set aside.

Of course, this distinction in terms is not always so clearly seen. Like the term "dating," the term "courting" may also be mistakenly viewed as a distinct category of relationship rather than an activity. I will talk more about this when I discuss some of the drawbacks to courting.

CONSERVATIVE BOUNDARIES

Typically, couples who choose to establish a courting relationship do so out of a desire to maintain physical purity. Young men and women who are willing to forgo the temporary pleasures of dating relationships until they are ready for a courting relationship tend to be serious about honoring God with their sexuality. Consequently, many courtships entail clearly established boundaries and place a strong emphasis on the need for sexual purity. Whether this conservative side of courting is a by-product of the maturity of those who choose to court or inherent within the system itself, courting is typically characterized by careful, safe relationships in which purity is given utmost attention. This need for sexual purity is not always given the same emphasis in casual dating relationships.

FAMILY INVOLVEMENT

Another positive aspect of courting is its emphasis on family (particularly parental) involvement. This emphasis stems from the idea that one's parents have the objectivity and wisdom to help determine the best spouse for their child. For many, the need for parental involvement is not merely an issue of wisdom and perspective but also authority. In other words, many believe that a daughter is under the authority of her father until such time as she comes under the authority of her husband. The father's involvement in the process then is not just a good idea but is an essential element of his fatherly responsibility. The daughter, therefore, submits to her father's spiritual authority in his approval or disapproval of a prospective husband.[1]

Parental involvement also acts as accountability. The courting couple spends a great deal of time with their families, which helps to maintain purity and also provides an opportunity for the two individuals to see their prospective spouses in a comfortable, authentic environment.

A GODLY OBJECTIVE

Perhaps the most advantageous aspect of courting is its objective. Unlike many dating relationships, the goal of courtship is marriage. This helps to secure a godly objective in the pursuing of romantic and sexual satisfaction. The young person who renounces casual dating and embraces courtship will be spared much of the pain that can come from misplaced trust and premature expressions of sexuality and romance.

A commitment to courting, for instance, will prevent a sixteen-year-old from falling into these pitfalls, for he will maintain familial relationships with the women in his life until he is able to actually pursue the true objective for which the erotic aspect of his sexuality was primarily created. Marriage, then, is clearly held forth as the goal of sexual and romantic expression. This desire to reserve sexuality and romance until it can find its full expression in marriage is extremely valuable in protecting the image of God.

COURTING CONS

In many respects, the Non-Approach is essentially courting without the formality. The Non-Approach's lack of formality was intentional. Though few functional distinctions may exist between these two concepts, the formality of courting relationships is a concern to me. Though I readily affirm that courting is a better alternative to finding a spouse than dating, I believe the formalness of a courting relationship makes it possible to be wrongly viewed as a legitimate, distinct category of male/female relationships. To simply exchange one man-made category of relationship for another will not serve us well in the long-term. Following are a few potential dangers that may be associated with some types of courting relationships.

COURTING AS A CATEGORY OF RELATIONSHIP

The exclusivity of a courting relationship can become problematic. It can strongly imply that a courting couple possesses a relationship that is distinct from their other relationships with members of the opposite sex. (For instance, we would not typically think of a courting couple as "just friends.") This can lead to the mistaken impression that a courting couple is outside the guidelines governing the sexual and romantic expression found in the Neighbor Relationship. Obvious dangers then arise concerning both physical and emotional purity.

As much as courting is dating with the goal of marriage in mind, and by dating we mean the *activity* of going on dates, then courting can fit within the framework of the God-ordained male/female relationships. But if "dating with a purpose" refers to establishing *a distinct category of relationship,* then courting is open to the same criticism that we discussed regarding dating in chapters 3 and 4. The pitfalls of dating do not simply endanger those who are not ready for marriage but all people who would enter into such a relationship with the conscious (or unconscious) belief that this type of relationship absolved them of the guidelines of purity that exist within the Neighbor Relationship.

Devoid of Permanency

Like dating, a courtship involves no real promise or commitment. It simply entails the commitment to develop a relationship until one or the other no longer desires to develop the relationship. Like a dating relationship, courtship is essentially a paper house. It has the language (couple, pair, etc.) and form of a marriage relationship, but it lacks the commitment and permanency of a marriage relationship. No one has really promised anything.

If this view is understood from the outset, the dangers of courting are decreased. But when a couple begins to think that a courtship entails some form of relationship that is distinct from the Neighbor Relationship, they can begin to unconsciously assume that it is now safe to begin moving in some of their emotional/romantic furniture. But this breaks with the image of God, specifically Christ's relationship with the church. A dating relationship nor a courtship offers permanency. By placing a title on a relationship, such as "courting" or "dating," this lack of permanency is often masked.

The Difficulty of Romantic Purity

The potential emotional/romantic intensity of a courtship that can result from the mistaken notion of permanency is another area of concern. While talking with a father about this book, he related his experience of a young man who called him to ask permission to court his daughter. His daughter was away at college and he had never met the young man. He was unfamiliar with the concept of courting and found the young man's question a bit unsettling. He couldn't help but feel like this was a rather big deal, and he wasn't so sure he wanted to bestow his blessing upon such an intense relationship without having any knowledge of the young man.

This father's reservation speaks to the seriousness of a courting relationship. It is not just another relationship. Because of this, I believe a courting couple could find it difficult to maintain the romantic purity that the Neighbor Relationship dictates. As mentioned, most courting couples have high standards regarding the physical relationship, but the need to maintain romantic purity can be more easily overlooked within a courting relationship. A courtship should not be an occasion to fall in love as much as an opportunity to see if falling in love within the context of marriage is possible. But the intensity and exclusiveness of a courtship can make it difficult to keep from crossing these emotional boundaries.

The Future Evolution of Terms

As we mentioned earlier in chapter 3, the term "dating" has evolved over the years to mean something different than it did in the past. In the past, dating was viewed in much the same way as courtship is viewed today. By this I mean that the term "dating" did not describe a category of relationship as much as it described an activity.

I have found that when talking to my parents' generation about the basic principles of this book, they have not immediately seen the danger in establishing dating relationships. For them, the activity of dating did not grant a special dispensation of freedom from the guidelines that were otherwise dictated in the Neighbor Relationship. In other words, my parents' generation thought of dating primarily as an activity, not as a kind of relationship. (Rather, they used the term "going steady" to describe what we now call "dating.") For many within my parents' generation, having a physical relationship with someone you were merely dating was improper.

But the term "dating" has evolved in meaning since then, and I am concerned that a similar shift of meaning could also happen over time with the term "courting." And when courting comes to be viewed as a category of relationship separate from the Neighbor Relationship, the objective standards of sexual purity are in jeopardy. It will do us little good to replace the man-made category of Dating with the man-made category of Courting.

Though most courting couples have high standards regarding sexual purity, I fear that if a courting relationship is viewed as separate from the Neighbor Relationship, it will be only a matter of time until those standards are laid aside. If the standards of sexual purity do not stem from our understanding of the Bible, they are doomed to slide into obscurity.

Conclusion

Courtship has many advantages over the typical dating system. But I fear that it can too easily be mistaken as a legitimate form of male/female relationship separate from the Neighbor Relationship. Any system that appears to separate a couple from the Neighbor Relationship has potential to separate them from its guidelines of sexual and emotional purity as well.

In light of this, I would strongly caution those who choose to court to remember that even within a courtship, a couple is bound to the romantic and physical purity that is dictated by the Neighbor Relationship. In the end, courting is really no better than dating if it does not help a man and a woman maintain the boundaries that God has prescribed.

WORKS REFERENCED

Clark, Jeramy. *I Gave Dating a Chance: A Biblical Perspective to Balance the Extremes.* Colorado Springs, CO: WaterBrook Press, 2001.

Harris, Joshua. *Boy Meets Girl.* Sisters, OR: Multnomah Press, 2000.

_____. *I Kissed Dating Goodbye.* Sisters, OR: Multnomah Press, 1997.

Holzmann, John. *Dating with Integrity.* Dallas: Word Publishing, 1992.

Kimnach, Wilson H., Kenneth P. Minkema, and Douglas A. Sweeney, eds. "The Excellency of Christ." *The Sermons of Jonathan Edwards: A Reader.* New Haven and London: Yale University Press, 1999.

MacArthur, John. *The MacArthur New Testament Commentary: Matthew 1—7.* Chicago: Moody Press, 1985.

McDowell, Josh, and Bob Hostetler. *Right from Wrong: What You Need to Know to Help Youth Make Right Choices.* Dallas: Word Publishing, 1994.

Phillips, Michael and Judy Phillips. *Best Friends for Life: An Extraordinary New Approach to Dating, Courtship, and Marriage—for Parents and Their Teens.* Minneapolis: Bethany House Publishers, 1997.

Ruppert, Martha. *The Dating Trap: Helping Your Children Make Wise Choices in Their Relationships.* Chicago: Moody Press, 2000.

Willard, Dallas. *The Divine Conspiracy: Rediscovering Our Hidden Life in God.* San Francisco: Harper Collins, 1998.

NOTES

CHAPTER 1

[1] Jonathan Edwards, who saw all of earthly life as an illustration of heavenly realities, also saw marriage as an illustration of our spiritual marriage with Christ. He wrote, "[Christ is] united to you by a spiritual union, so close *as to be fitly represented by the union of the wife to the husband,* of the branch to the vine, of the member to the head; yea, so as to be one spirit" (emphasis added; Wilson H. Kimnach, Kenneth P. Minkema, and Douglas A. Sweeney, eds., "The Excellency of Christ," *The Sermons of Jonathan Edwards: A Reader* [New Haven and London: Yale University Press, 1999], 186).

Augustine also saw marriage as a fitting type of Christ and the church. He wrote, "It is of Christ and the Church that this is most truly understood: 'And they twain shall be one flesh' " (Philip Schaff, "On Forgiveness of Sins and Baptism," *Saint Augustine: Anti-Pelagian Writings: A Select Library of the Nicence and Post-Nicene Fathers of the Christian Church* [Edinburgh: T&T Clark; Grand Rapids: Wm. B. Eerdmans Publishing Company, 1997]. But in keeping with his day, Augustine did not have a high view of marriage and sex themselves. In my estimation, his position on sex was inconsistent with the rest of his theology, which held generally that everything God created was good and to be enjoyed with thanksgiving.

[2] I have chosen to follow the Revised Standard Version's rendering of this verse, which translates the conjunction *de* ("*and* I am speaking," v. 32) as "and" rather than "but" (per NIV and NASB). The point that Paul is making here is that the mystery of oneness is really about Christ and his relationship with the church even more than it is about earthly marriage. It is not as though Paul changed subjects from Christ and the church to a man and his wife, but suddenly caught himself by saying, "But where was I? Oh, yes. . . . I was talking about Christ and the church." Rather, he is trying to demonstrate that the one-flesh relationship that exists between a man and a woman (ordained in Genesis 2:24) is really about Christ and the church. In other words, to speak of human marriage is to speak of Christ and

the church.

[3] The fact that Paul uses a passage from Genesis to refer to Christ and the church is not inconsistent with its use in its original context. Many times throughout Scripture one verse applies to many situations. An example of this can be seen in Matthew 2:15, where the apostle mentions Christ's journey to Egypt as a small child to be a fulfillment of an Old Testament prophecy in Hosea 11:1. In the Old Testament context, the Hosea passage would have been understood as a reference to the Exodus. But Matthew saw in that passage an even deeper fulfillment as it applied to Christ. Paul is using the same technique here, showing that the ultimate purpose of sex and marriage is seen with the coming of Christ.

[4] First Corinthians 6:15-17 highlights this same truth as well. Just as in the Ephesians passage, Paul demonstrates here that sexual intercourse serves as a living image of our unseen union with Christ.

The term "one flesh" in this passage is used to refer specifically to sexual intercourse. Further, Paul's command regarding sexual purity is based on the oneness that exists in the Christian's relationship with Christ. We are called to abstain from becoming one with a prostitute because we have already become one with Christ (v. 17). We have become one with him on a spiritual plane, just as a man and a prostitute become one on a physical plane. The physical oneness then that results from sex serves as an image of the spiritual oneness that results from our union with Christ.

[5] Dallas Willard makes similar critiques regarding the current evangelical understanding of the gospel in his book *The Divine Conspiracy: Rediscovering Our Hidden Life in God* (San Francisco: Harper Collins, 1998, pp. 35-50). He even notes his own displeasure with the same bumper sticker I mention. Though not agreeing with all of his solutions, I nonetheless affirm his recognition of the problem.

[6] For further implications of the truth that God created sex to serve as a living image of the gospel, see Appendix B.

Chapter 2

[1] Jeramy Clark, *I Gave Dating a Chance: A Biblical Perspective to Balance the Extremes* (Colorado Springs: WaterBrook Press, 2001), 108, 109.

[2] Josh McDowell and Bob Hostetler, *Right from Wrong* (Dallas: Word Publishing, 1994), 270, 271.

[3] God has not spelled out clearly why he put a decisive end to interfamily sexual relations. I am convinced, however, that this command also relates specifically to the image of God. The Old Testament Law (of which the command in discussion is a part) was established as a means by which God could dwell among his people in an elevated way. Prior to the Law, God did not dwell among his people in any kind of permanent capacity. The Law was given that the people might know how to behave in such a way that God could live in their midst without destroying them for their sin. So through the external purity afforded by the Law, God took up residence among his people in a way that he had never done before. This new relationship, in fact, served as a foreshadowing of Christ's relationship to the church. It is not a coincidence that God's commands regarding interfamily relations were given at the same time this new quality of relationship was established. Perhaps human sexuality then somehow reflects the establishment of this unique new relationship.

Notice in Leviticus 18:10 the reason God prohibits sex between grandparent and grandchild: " 'The nakedness of your son's daughter or your daughter's daughter, their nakedness you shall not uncover; *for their nakedness is yours*' " (NASB). In other words, God prohibits sex between grandparent and grandchild because it is essentially like having sex with yourself. The phrase "their nakedness" at the end of this verse could refer either to the grandparent's child or directly to the grandchild. Either way, the reasoning is the same. A man's child is his very image, his own nature. So a man's child is the image of both the man and the man's father, in whose image the man was born. Thus, to have sex with one's child or grandchild is to have sex with one's own image, one's own nature.

But why did God choose to prohibit uncovering one's own na-kedness in conjunction with the new relationship he was establish-ing with his people through the law? When blood relatives come together sexually, it essentially shows the union of like natures. But when two people from different families come together sexually, it demonstrates the union of two dissimilar natures. Ultimately then, it would seem that God has abolished sex between blood relatives because it does not portray the image of the union of two dissimilar natures, the very thing that the Law foreshadowed that was fulfilled in Christ.

[4] The NIV inserts the verb "treat" to make the passage more readable. The main positive verb is to "exhort" or "encourage," and the passage literally reads, "An older man do not rebuke, but rather encourage him as a father, younger men as brothers, older women as mothers, and younger women as sisters, in all purity." At its base then, the command is for Timothy to "encourage" (or exercise pasto-ral care) toward the women of his church as though they were his mother or sisters.

[5] Though the Greek word *agnos* may be used in a nonsexual context, it is used frequently in the New Testament to refer to sexual purity and has this meaning when referring to male/female relation-ships [see 2 Corinthians 11:2, 1 Peter 3:2, and Titus 2:5].

[6] John Holzmann also argues for this standard of purity in his book *Dating with Integrity* (Dallas: Word Publishing, 1992), 79, as does Martha Ruppert in her book *The Dating Trap: Helping Your Children Make Wise Choices in Their Relationships* (Chicago: Moody Press, 2000), 58–60.

[7] See William Graham Cole, *Sex and Love in the Bible* (New York: Association Press, 1959), 235.

Chapter 5

[1] The desire that Christ is referring to is clearly sexual. When a man has sexual desire for a woman who is not his spouse, he has

committed the sin of lust. We will discuss at the end of the chapter how it is possible to desire a woman (or man) as a future spouse without entering into the sin of lust.

[2] See Dallas Willard, *The Divine Conspiracy: Rediscovering Our Hidden Life in God* (San Francisco: Harper Collins, 1998) pp. 164-65, and John MacArthur, *The MacArthur New Testament Commentary, Matthew 1—7,* (Chicago: Moody Press, 1985), 302-03. Though in my mind both Willard and MacArthur rightly capture the overall spirit of the Sermon on the Mount, they do not seem to apply its teaching consistently in the area of sexual desire. The main point of debate involves the Greek preposition *pros,* which both Willard and MacArthur translate as "with a view to," thus the translation, "everyone who looks on a woman *with the intent* of lusting for her." Though this is a legitimate translation, *pros* can also be used to show a close connection between things, thus the translation, "everyone who looks on a woman *with regard to* lusting for her."

In this later translation (which I affirm), the emphasis is upon a *certain kind* of looking (the kind that includes sexual desire) and does not provide an exception clause if the aforementioned looking was not intentional. Even were we to grant the translation affirmed by Willard and MacArthur, it is by no means certain that Christ intended to excuse spontaneous lusting and meant to address only premeditated sexual desire. Such an argument rests upon silence. The context strongly steers us away from such a view.

[3] Dannah Gresh, *The Fashion Battle: Is It One Worth Fighting?* CBN.com, The Christian Broadcasting Network, March 1, 2004. In fairness to Gresh, the context of her statements shows that she is not trying to excuse men but to inform women of the need for appropriate dress and modesty. Though her intentions are pure, I feel that relying on this line of reasoning minimizes the power of the gospel to change a person's *desires* (as well as will) and neglects a positive reason for modesty. The motivation for modesty should stem chiefly from a desire to protect the image of God within human sexuality, not primarily as a means to help men refrain from lust. Even elderly women should dress modestly.

[4] In the same way, even in normal, healthy marriage relationships, the stimuli required to arouse sexual desire must be increased as the relationship progresses. A prolonged kiss does not necessarily produce the same intense sexual arousal that it likely did in the early days of the relationship. I believe this relates to the fact that we become increasingly aware that a sexual relationship with our spouse is not the all-satisfying answer to the ultimate longings of our soul. Prior to sexual intercourse, we find it easy to mistakenly suppose that such an encounter will be the ultimate experience—life fully lived. But as time wears on, we realize that though the sexual relationship is filled with meaning, it cannot serve as the ultimate fulfillment of our deepest desires. Prior to our first sexual relationship, we wrongly perceive that life's deepest needs can and will be met in that relationship; thus we are extremely aroused by even the slightest suggestion of sex. But after we have drunk deeply of that cup, our perception regarding its ability to meet our deepest needs begins to become a bit more realistic. We do not gravitate toward a sexual encounter with the same intensity, because our perception of its ability to satisfy our deepest longings has changed.

CHAPTER 6

[1] I have chosen to use the NIV rendering of this verse because I believe it most clearly captures the intent of the passage. The NASB, for example, translates this verse as, "That you will not arouse or awaken *my* love, until she pleases." The NASB's translation does not seem to fit the context as readily here as the NIV. It is hard to understand why the bride would be charging the young virgins not to arouse or awaken *her* love, when this is exactly what she is already rejoicing in. Further, translators of the NASB added the pronoun "my" for clarification; it is not part of the Hebrew text.

[2] See Revelation 19:1-9. The wedding of Christ and the church takes place upon his return. See also Revelation 21:1-3.

Chapter 7

[1] Appendix C addresses the issue of courting as another method of spouse finding. I find courting to be a more viable alternative to dating, but this method is not without its own potential problems. Like dating, courting runs the risk of becoming viewed as its own category of relationship, separate and distinct from the Neighbor Relationship.

Chapter 8

[1] Much of evangelical theology views the Old Testament Law as serving primarily as a means of highlighting our sinfulness. Though I believe the Law does serve this function, it seems short-sighted in light of many of Paul's comments in Galatians.

Chapter 9

[1] Prior to the Fall, clothing was unnecessary, for all of life was lived as sacred, devoted to God and untainted by sin and selfish desires. But when sin entered the world, our sexuality could not be freely manifested, for the world in which we live no longer images forth a pure reflection of God. In keeping with our fine china analogy, it is proper to say that before the Fall, every occasion was a sacred occasion, unabused and pure. Thus, there was no need to protect our sexuality. And though I have been talking about the sacredness of sexuality, it is not wrong to view the necessity of clothing after the Fall as a statement about our own condition of sinfulness. Prior to the coming of Christ, our inner and deepest self was still dead in sin. To this extent, our sexuality bore the marks of death, and indeed there was a legitimate shame upon it—not because sexuality itself was shameful, but because of our fallenness that tainted it. But with the coming of Christ, our inner man has been redeemed. No longer do we need to feel shame about the deepest parts of ourselves. Yet as the world in which we live is still unredeemed, it is necessary to protect as sacred that which truly has become such.

[2] Many excellent resources are available for parents that provide detailed information regarding the content of movies. My wife and I

use www.kidsinmind.com to preview the content of a movie before we see it. The site gives a rating for three categories: sex and nudity, violence, and profanity. It further details the exact nature of the ratings so a viewer is able to judge the appropriateness of a movie.

[3] Some shows or movies, however, are inappropriate for children but are proper for adults. The news might be an example of this. Though we as parents might watch the news, we should probably not thrust the reality of the world's depravity upon our children at too early of an age. Historical war movies might be similar. But news and historical programs deal with realities. They are truths of the world that we as adults must come to terms with. We don't watch the horror of war or hear the news of a rape for entertainment purposes. Our children can sense this difference. For instance, though both contain violence, I would not place an action movie full of gratuitous violence in the same company as an authentic and realistic war movie. The first has little redeeming value. The second forces us to come to grips with the reality of our history and the cost that was paid in blood by the men who serve our country. War movies are meant to be sobering, not entertaining.

APPENDIX A

[1] Dallas Willard makes similar critiques regarding the current evangelical understanding of the gospel in his book *The Divine Conspiracy*, 35–50.

APPENDIX C

[1] Though I believe this line of reasoning has merit, particularly while a daughter is living under her parents' roof, I do not see Scripture necessitating that a woman cannot live on her own apart from the headship of a man. (See Numbers 27:1–7: At the time of this account, the daughters of Zelophehad were not married, as is shown in Numbers 36:1–3.) Depending upon her age and place in life, her father's role in her life gradually moves from that of formal authority to informal influence.